Subsistence Farming in Roman Italy

1. Shepherd milking a goat, from a sarcophagus in the Museo Nazionale, Rome. (A third-century motif. cf. *Repertorium der Christlich-Antiken Sarcophage*, I, no. 988. Deutsches Archäologisches Institut). Note the reed shelter, the milking position and the wicker stool.

Joan M. Frayn

Subsistence Farming in Roman Italy

Centaur Press Limited
1979

First published 1979 by Centaur Press Ltd.
Fontwell, Sussex, and 11-14 Stanhope Mews West,
London, S.W.7.
ISBN 0-90000092 9

Printed in Great Britain by
Villiers Publications Ltd., London, N.W.5.

CONTENTS

ILLUSTRATIONS

Acknowledgements

I am indebted to many people for assistance of various kinds in the preparation of this book. In particular, I should like to thank Dr. D. Whitehouse, the Director of the British School at Rome, and his staff, and the Librarian and staff of the Library of the Hellenic and Roman Societies in London. I am most grateful to Professor K. D. White for providing a Foreword to the book, and to Professor P. A. Brunt of Brasenose College, Oxford, and Mr J. V. Muir of the Department of Education, King's College, London, for their help and encouragement. I should also like to express my gratitude here for a grant from the Hugh Last Fund of the Society for the Promotion of Roman Studies toward the cost of the illustrations.

J. M. Frayn

Sources of the Illustrations

1. The Mansell Collection.
2. Rivista geografica italiana, Florence.
3. ENIT Roma.
4. ENIT Roma.
5. L'Antiquité classique, Louvain.
6. Accademia Nazionale dei Lincei (Alberto Davico).
7. The British School at Rome (G. D. B. Jones).
8. The British School at Rome (G. D. B. Jones).

The author and publishers acknowledge with thanks permission from the following for quotations made in the text:
Basil Blackwell: Landscape and History in Central Italy, J. B. Ward Perkins.
Cambridge University Press: Samnium and the Samnites, E. T.

Salmon. The Economy of the Roman Empire, R. Duncan-Jones.

Walter de Gruyter, Berlin: Tiberius Gracchus and the Beginning of the Roman Revolution, E. Badian.

The Organisation for Economic Cooperation and Development, Paris: Agricultural Policy Report.

Penguin Books Ltd: The Letters of the Younger Pliny, trans. B. Radice.

The Swedish Institute in Rome. The Iron Age Culture of Latium, Vol. I, P. G. Gierow.

Thames and Hudson Ltd: Roman Colonisation, E. T. Salmon. The Land Question and European Society, F. E. Huggett.

Van Gorcum & Co., Assen. Landscape in Romano-Campanian Mural Painting, W. J. T. Peters.

Foreword by Professor K. D. White

The ultimate aim of every social historian is to bring the past to life. For the student of the agrarian history of ancient Italy the task is particularly hazardous and daunting; to bring the ancient Italian farmer back to life involves a great variety of activities on the part of workers in many different and specialised disciplines, from lexicography to field archaeology, and from palaeobotany to pedology. Some of us have been engaged in the preliminary but highly necessary tasks of clearing away the undergrowth, and of finding, collecting and re-assembling the dead bones, others that of putting on the flesh.

Dr. Frayn belongs to this second group, and her book is devoted to the activities of that ubiquitous but overlooked feature of the landscape, the subsistence farmer. Hers is certainly no easy task; before Rome had become a world power, the Italian smallholder was already being enmeshed within a web of mythologising fantasy, while the real peasant, so we are told, was on the way to extinction as a result of the growth of slave-run *latifundia*. This once fashionable thesis has come in for severe criticism in recent years, and the latest excavations of farm sites in the Deep South and in Sicily are giving increasing support to the view that small mixed farming continued to flourish until well into the Empire, in those very areas that were supposedly taken over by *latifundia*.

Dr. Frayn's book, a work of synthesis and reconstruction, appears at an opportune moment — at one of those necessary pauses, when we down tools and survey the ground covered so far. The writer is well qualified for the task, for she brings to it a deep love of the classics, a lifetime's experience as a teacher, and an experience of the ways of country folk in those parts of Italy where old traditions of country life still persist, against a background of accelerating economic and social reform which, as she declares, will make it 'increasingly difficult for those who have never known rural life in its simpler forms to interpret even the literary evidence' (page 13).

This comprehensive, scholarly and fascinating survey deserves a wide readership. I commend it most warmly.

K. D. White
Edinburgh

LAND MEASURES

Ancient

1 iugerum	=	28,800 sq feet (240 × 120)

or, in terms of larger land measures:

1 iugerum	=	$\frac{5}{8}$ acre (0.25 ha)

Modern

1 hectare (ha)	=	2.47106 acres
1 acre	=	0.4047 ha.
1 ha.	=	10,000 sq metres
100 ha.	=	1 sq km

ABBREVIATIONS

The following abbreviations will be used:

CEHE *Cambridge Economic History of Europe*. ed. M. M. Postan and H. J. Habakkuk. Cambridge, 1971.

CIL *Corpus Inscriptionum Latinarum*.

ILLR *Inscriptiones Latinae Liberae Rei Publicae*.

JRS *Journal of Roman Studies*.

OECD *Organisation for Economic Cooperation and Development*.

PBSR *Papers of the British School at Rome*.

ROL *Remains of Old Latin*. ed. E. H. Warmington. London, 1940.

Introduction

Before discussing in detail the life and work of the poorer country-folk of Roman Italy we must consider the progress which has recently been made in the study of Roman agriculture in general. With the publication in 1970 of *Roman Farming* by K. D. White, a modern and definitive work on the subject has for the first time been made available in this country. The forerunner of *Roman Farming*, though very different in style and treatment, was W. E. Heitland's *Agricola*, published in 1921, only part of which was concerned with Italy. It was not the purpose of either of these writers to discuss in detail the life and work of the peasant proprietor or tenant. Heitland, as he indicated in the sub-title of his book, was studying Greco-Roman agriculture 'from the point of view of labour', and by 'labour' he meant employees, especially slaves. K. D. White's book is devoted chiefly to the economy of the villa and to the process of farming on a commercial basis, these being the subjects upon which the most written evidence is available. They are also probably the most important aspects of Roman farming for those studying the literature of the Augustan age and the early Empire.

The activities of those farming at subsistence level in Italy in the Roman period are often regarded today in the same manner as they were by Heitland when he wrote:

'But just for a moment the veil is lifted to remind us that in the upland districts there was still an Italy agriculturally, as socially, very different from the lowland arable of which we generally think when speaking of Italian farming . . . It is to be regretted that we have so little evidence as to the condition of the dalesmen, other than the passages of such writers as Horace and Juvenal, who refer to them as rustic folk a sojourn among whom is a refreshing experience after the noise and bustle of Rome . . . But to get a true picture of the country as a whole is, in the absence of statistics, not possible.' (Heitland, op. cit., pp. 284-5.)

It is our intention in the chapters which follow to try to 'lift the veil' a little further from the face of the ancient Italian countryside, and to glimpse as fully as possible the life of the peasantry in Roman times. We shall probably never be able now to reconstruct that life with any degree of certainty, but it is particularly desirable to make the attempt at the present time. The old agricultural ways are still pursued to a greater or lesser extent in various parts of Italy and her islands. However, with the acceleration of change in the modern world not many traces of ancient rural customs will remain to be studied by later generations than our own. Moreover it will become increasingly difficult for those who have never known rural life in its simpler forms to interpret even the literary evidence available.

There is no lack of literary material to illustrate this subject as almost every Roman writer at some time refers to country life. This is true even of such 'men about town' as Juvenal and Persius. But can we rely upon the evidence of the poets, or are they giving us an idealised picture of the countryside? Virgil might be particularly suspect, since he is often said to have been supporting Augustus' programme of reform. Yet few works on agriculture list more pests and disasters which can beset the farmer than are to be found in the *Georgics* of Virgil. Geese and cranes will attack the crops; the farmers must wage continual war on weeds; field-mice and voles will spoil the threshing-floor; weevils will infest the granary and goats will eat the young vines. As for the weather, there will be a drought in summer, and storms of wind, hail, snow and rain in the winter. If nothing else destroys the crops, they may be accidentally set on fire. If Virgil were trying to show farming as a pleasant and easy occupation he would surely have omitted some of these details. Instead he continually emphasises the 'labor improbus' which is demanded of the countryman and seems not so much to be idealising the processes of agriculture as trying to raise their status in the eyes of gentlemen. The Elder Pliny, for all his admiration of the poet, felt obliged to comment on this and to state his own rather different attitude (*N.H.* XIV, 1 (7)): 'sed nos oblitterata quoque scrutabimur, nec deterrebit quarundam rerum humilitas'. While we must consider a writer's purpose and how it may affect the presentation of his material, the test of all Roman writing upon country life must be twofold. Do the writer's facts generally tally with those given by other ancient sources? Are they probable in view of what we know of Italy before, during and after the Roman period? Not only each author but each passage must be examined with reference to such criteria, and when this is done much valuable information emerges.

With the prose writers we should be on firmer ground but here other difficulties arise. No Roman author whose work has come down to us is concerned with the economics of Italian agriculture as a whole. The agronomists, Cato, Varro and Columella are discussing the management of an individual estate or farm. Palladius offers us a compendium of miscellaneous advice on agriculture, mainly connected with the villa economy of the Empire, but including interesting items which clearly have a different origin. All these writers, and likewise the Elder Pliny in his *Naturalis Historia* sometimes refer specifically to an ancient or rustic procedure. Even when this is not explicitly stated, one can often identify such material among the more sophisticated ideas being presented. For other Roman writers agrarian problems are only incidental, though in a political or legal context they may be discussed at some length.

At the present time we are not entirely dependent upon the literary sources for our information. Archaeological research in Mediterranean countries and elsewhere is making available to us much new knowledge about ancient agriculture. Recent investigation of the Apennine and other pre-Roman cultures in Central

Italy, together with the development of Etruscan archaeology, offers a sound basis for consideration of early Roman settlement. The discovery of centuriation grids, the re-examination of the work of the *agrimensores* and the mapping of Roman roads in Italy have added to the evidence for the life of the country-dweller as well as the townsman. Regional studies by Italian scholars, and detailed surveys of particular areas such as those undertaken by the British School at Rome have illumined many aspects of life in the Roman period concerning which little evidence was available before. It is proposed to make use of such material here side by side with the literary texts, wherever it seems relevant.

II

As a basis for our study of subsistence farming in Roman Italy we must define more precisely the type of farm under consideration. If we adopt the classification made by K. D. White (op. cit., p. 387) we are chiefly concerned here with his first and lowest category, the smallholding (10-80 *iugera*). As we shall see, however, there is reason to believe that many Romans and Italians, even members of certain colonies, owned less than 10 *iugera*, some perhaps only possessing the traditional *heredium* of 2 *iugera*. At the same time the upper limit of 80 *iugera* will not be too rigidly observed, because many facts concerning farms slightly larger than this may be applicable also to the smaller holdings. Tenants, colonists and employees will be discussed as well as owner-occupiers, but only in so far as their activities are relevant to our main theme, farming at subsistence level. Many of these small plots of land, containing as they often did the dwelling house and the family grave in addition to the arable, can hardly be described by the English word 'farm': to the Roman such a plot was an *agellus** or a *fundus*, unless he preferred to state the size of it or dismiss it as *pauca iugera*. The word 'farm' may however be used here for convenience to include even the smallest

---

* Varro, *Res Rusticae*, III, 16, considers that an *agellus* is not more than one *iugerum*, but the word was not always used so exactly.

holdings. The countrymen whom we are studying were often called in Latin *agrestes, rustici,* or since many, though not all, of them lived in the uplands, *montani.* These peasant farmers cultivated their land for their own subsistence and usually had little or no surplus beyond their own and their families' requirements. If they engaged in barter or trade it was in order to acquire those necessities of life which they could not produce on their own plot or obtain from the wild.

The period to which this study relates extends from the fifth century BC to the end of the second century AD. Evidence from earlier and later periods will be used for illustration and comparison. It would not seem practicable at such an early stage in the treatment of the subject to adopt stricter chronological limits. Moreover in discussing the countryside, where the pace of change is always slow, it seems desirable to take a broad view. Modes of life which were widespread in Italy during the pre-Roman Iron Age, for example, must have remained largely unchanged in early Roman times in the remoter regions owing to the difficulties of transport and communication. Similarly in later periods progress was slow in areas distant from urban centres.

III

We shall discuss first the type of countryside in which these peasant farmers lived and worked, the various land-holdings and their use, and the pastoralism which continued for some either instead of or in addition to the practice of agriculture. Colonisation and other political developments will be included in so far as they affected the small farmer. Sections are devoted to the buildings and equipment of the small-holding, the intention being to present the life of the *rustici* as farmers in as many aspects as possible. Their life as Roman citizens or soldiers, or members of tribes and municipalities has previously received much more attention than their farming activities. While allowing for the effect of political and social movements upon the small farmer, we wish to direct attention here chiefly to the details of his day-to-day existence in the rural environment.

CHAPTER ONE

The Smallholder and his Environment

At the time of the first settlement on the site of Rome both tradition and archaeological evidence suggest that small-scale agriculture and pastoralism were the basis of the economy of Rome itself and its immediate vicinity. A similar form of society existed throughout Latium in the sixth and seventh centuries BC, where it was characterised by a number of small, self-governing communities (*populi*) living around and within their village centres (*oppida*).[1] Some *populi* combined to form loose federations, chiefly in the first instance for religious purposes such as the worship of Diana at Aricia, and the gatherings at Lucus Feroniae.[2] Other such groupings were the *populi Albenses* and perhaps originally the *nomen Latinum* itself.[3] These arrangements imply the development of easy communications between settlements on the plain of Latium and along the Tiber valley at an early date. At least until the end of the fifth century BC these *oppida* appear to have been numerous and Latium a well-populated area. According to Pliny (*N.H.* III, 5 (68-70)) fifty-three ancient cities of Latium had disappeared without trace: although this passage presents difficulties of interpretation in detail, its general import is clear, namely that there had once been far more settlements in Latium than were in existence in the first century AD.[4] By that time the suburban area of Rome was occupied by the villas of the richer citizens and development of this kind extended over the more attractive parts of the plain and the low hills. The coastal region, less populous because of its marshy hinterland, was occupied by villagers who were engaged in agriculture, seafaring, fishing and the salt trade.

According to our literary sources Central Italy in the fifth century BC was inhabited by a number of distinct tribal groups. The names of many of these continued to be associated with certain tracts of country at least until the end of the Republican era. Livy, looking back at the history of the fourth and fifth centuries BC writes of the Sabines, the Samnites, the Umbri and many more. Strabo, although he is writing of the situation as he knew it long after the Romans had gained political and military control of Italy, assumes that these tribal names can still be used to describe the inhabitants of the interior. He only comments on the matter when, as in the case of the Falisci (V, 2, 9) there is any doubt about their identity.[5] The Etruscans are also still a distinct group in Strabo's account, 'τρίτοι δ'εἰσὶ συνεχεῖς τούτοις οἱ Τυρρηνοί, τὰ πεδία ἔχοντες τὰ μέχρι τοῦ ποταμοῦ τοῦ Τιβέριδος,' he writes (V, 2, 1) after he has discussed the Ligures further north. 'Τυρρηνοὶ δὲ παύονται ὑπ'αὐτοῖς τοῖς ὄρεσι τοῖς περικλείουσιν ἐκ τῆς Λιγυστικῆς εἰς τὸν Ἀδρίαν . . . .' He endeavours to describe exactly the territorial basis of each of the peoples he mentions, and although antiquarian interests play a part here, these boundaries must to some extent have been acknowledged by Strabo's contemporaries if his treatment of the subject-matter was to be intelligible to them. During the period we are discussing these groups, particularly in the remoter districts seem to have retained many features of their distinctive cultures long after they became subject to the political and military power of Rome.

Throughout Central Italy an economy based on the village and the small farm continued at least until the end of the fourth century BC. Livy, IX, 13, 5, referring to the year 318 BC, writes of the Samnites 'ea tempestate in montibus vicatim habitantes' E. T. Salmon in *Samnium and the Samnites*, p. 77, develops this theme:

'Theirs was a typical subsistence economy in which each *pagus* had to rely on its own resources for the basic necessities of life, food, clothing and materials for housing.'

A contrast between urban and rural life in these regions is implied in Livy X, 17, 1. The consul, P. Decius, in 296 BC, 'Quid per agros, inquit, vagamus vicatim circumferentes bellum? quin urbes et moenia adgredimur?' They did attack the cities, 'spe maioris quam ex agrestibus populationibus praedae'. Livy apparently considers that many of the Samnites were still living in *vici* at the beginning of the third century BC and that the country-dwellers could provide much less of value in the way of plunder than the townspeople: these were not wealthy farmsteads.

In Southern Italy the existence from the seventh and eighth centuries BC of Greek cities on the coast had encouraged commercial and social exchange along the littoral. Yet this commerce was confined to the coastal plains and the inland peoples were largely unaffected by it. This was especially true of mountainous regions, where a mode of life derived from and continuous with that of the Iron Age persisted throughout the Greek period (J. de la Genière, in *Le Genti non Greche della Magna Grecia*, p. 260). As regards Daunia, E. M. De Juliis (*Civiltà preistoriche e protoistoriche della Daunia*, p. 295) considers that on the present evidence it seems that in the fourth century BC the inhabitants of this area were just passing from a pre-urban society 'di tipo paganico' to one of a truly urban type. At this time also the Samnites were expanding in the direction of the coastal plains and pressing upon the inhabitants of Apulia.

A different situation existed in Campania. In Naples and its environs urban civilisation dated back to the foundation of the Greek colonies. The exceptional fertility of the land and its favourable climate encouraged viticulture and the growing of fruit and cereals. Access to maritime trade, and later the building of Roman roads, such as the Via Appia and the Via Latina, assisted in making this a most prosperous area of settlement, attractive to commercial exploitation. By the end of the Republic much of the land was farmed from *villae rusticae* or as market gardens, while on the coast itself villas designed for *otium* proliferated, especially during the early years of the Empire. Nevertheless Cicero (*De Lege Agraria*, II, 27, 73) implies that this countryside in the first century BC was occupied by farmers of moderate means: 'Totus enim ager Campanus colitur et possidetur a plebe, et a plebe optima et modestissima . . .' Recent archaeological discoveries indicate that small properties continued to exist in this area in the first century AD.[6]

The *pagus* and the *vicus* have already been mentioned, and there were other groupings to which the small farm might belong, such as *compita, fora* and *conciliabula*. Festus (*De Verborum Significatu*) derives *pagus* from the Doric παγαί and says 'pagi dicti a fontibus, quod eadem aqua uterentur'. It is used by Livy to denote a country district, and from it comes *Paganalia*, the rural festival. The *pagani* were 'countryfolk' or, as often in Tacitus, 'civilians'. Tacitus *Histories* III, 24, has been cited as an example of the second meaning, but it seems reasonable to conclude that it means the countryfolk as opposed to the urban *vulgus*. *Paganus* is becoming a term of disrespect at this time (cf. its use later by Christian writers). The following description of the *pagus* is given by E. T. Salmon (op. cit., p. 79):

'The *pagus* was an administrative sub-unit, the smallest such amongst the Italic peoples, but it was not a town: it was a district of variable size usually larger than a *fundus*, but smaller than a *territorium*, and might itself contain one or more settlements, either unwalled but stockaded villages (*vici*) where the country was flat, or walled citadels of refuge (*oppida, castella*) where the country was mountainous. Neither *vici* nor *oppida* seem to have had any political life of their own . . .'

The *compita* or cross-roads were important as the scene of certain religious rites, including the Compitalia in January,[7] and, at any rate from the later Republic onwards, some kind of public meeting place. Cicero (*De Lege Agraria, I, 7*) mentions the possibility of holding an auction 'in triviis aut in compitis', and Horace (*Epist. I, 1, 49*) refers to a boxer displaying his prowess 'circum pagos et circum compita.'[8] It is interesting to find René Dumont (*Types of Rural Economy*, p. 254) describing farms in the Maremma in modern times which are grouped together, each occupying one angle of a cross-roads. In other parts of Italy also two or three old farms may be observed at the junction of small, country roads. Can this sometimes be a relic of the *compita*? The siting of farms in this way would facilitate the sharing of equipment and workers. It should be remembered that the ancient meeting-points would have been at the junctions of by-roads or tracks which antedated the paved roads. When the Roman roads were established an attempt was made to provide a similar network of meeting-places and small communities based upon them. The *fora* and *conciliabula* which resulted were created for Roman citizens and became centres for purveying official information. Livy's phrase 'per fora atque conciliabula',[9] so often used in the context of proclamations and official notices, sounds like the preamble to an edict or the instruction to a town-crier. The *fora* were on the main roads and many of them grew into towns. The *conciliabula* were properly the new centres for the old tribal organisation of the countryside, though the word could be used less exactly, as in Livy VII, 15, 11. Neither of these centres had a political life of its own, and they had not, like the *coloniae* and the cities, a *territorium*.[10] Their only connection therefore with the agricultural activities of the small farmers would be as possible markets for their produce and for the purchase of such items as salt, metal goods, pitch and oil. Livy, XXIX, 37, 4, mentions the levying of the salt tax 'in foris et conciliabulis'.

At the end of the third century BC came the Punic Wars, during which large numbers of Roman citizens were absent from their farms for protracted terms of military service. The effects of Hannibal's invasion of Italy upon the smallholders are discussed below, in Chapter V, p. 80-1. It suffices to say here that the farming communities in Central and Southern Italy were reduced in numbers at this time, that the supply of free agricultural labourers diminished and the proportion of slave labour increased. It appears however, from Cato's instruction to the *vilicus* (V. 4) to employ different *operarii* and *mercennarii* each day that there was still a plentiful reserve of free labour at the time when he was writing. This remark of Cato seems to tally with his advice to the master in the previous chapter to be on good terms with his neighbours, because in that way he will be better able to put work out to contract and to obtain additional workers for himself. We have already seen the important part played by the small farmer during the early centuries of Rome's history: there must have remained a considerable number of small farms occupied by owners or tenants during the first and second centuries BC and later. Southern Etruria is an area which has received considerable attention lately and G. D. B. Jones writes of it: [11] 'One of the most valuable results of archaeological survey has been to emphasise the extent of the small-holdings, especially in the late Republican period. In the northern Ager Veientanus, the western Ager Faliscus and the southern Ager Capenas, for instance, there are extensive settlements of the late Republican period. The small farms which compose them are datable from the Campanian black-glaze pottery found on them and in the densest area north of Veii, for instance, examples occur every few hundred yards.' Conclusions drawn from field surveys in South Etruria and elsewhere have been subject to criticism recently on the ground that these small sites may not represent independent units, but buildings belonging to one large establishment. If, as would appear from the details, some of them are working farms on which a family or group of workers lived as tenants of a landowner, they represent at any rate a survival of the traditional small-scale undertaking. If they were merely industrial sites or storehouses or slave-barracks they would not have any relevance to our present consideration. Strabo makes frequent reference to Italian peoples living κωμηδνό in his own day,[12] and Livy echoes this word with his *vicatim*. These adverbs, as also Livy's *pagatim*,[13] recall the ancient Italian way of life, with small farms grouped in unfortified villages or country districts. They are not without meaning even in the economic sphere, for there is a marked difference between the *urbes* of Latium and the coastal region in general and the *pagi* of the interior. Even if the inhabitants of an *urbs* went out to work in the fields each day, as they still do in some parts of Italy, the urban centre formed a larger unit for commerce and attracted specialist craftsmen. The proportion of those engaged in non-agricultural pursuits increased, thus gradually changing the pattern of the local economy.

The old order had been preserved for a long time in some areas of the countryside owing to the nature of the terrain. While in the vicinity of Rome and on the plains of Latium and Campania communication between farms was comparatively easy, the mountains and forests elsewhere caused a long-continued separation and isolation. Differences of climate increased the sense of regional particularity which is still noticeable today.[14] Four-fifths of Italy consists of mountains and hill-country, and much of the remainder was marshy in ancient times. Even on the plains communication was not always easy, as is suggested by Livy's mention in VIII, 14, 10, of rewards for the people of Fundi and Formiae 'quod per fines eorum tuta pacataque semper erat via.' These communities on the route of the future Appian Way, had been willing to allow free passage through their territory, but what of the others? This incident concerns the passage of military forces and people on other official errands, many of them travelling long distances, as they could do more easily later on the Roman roads. Communication for the small farmer and for countryfolk in general was a different matter.

J. B. Ward Perkins (*Landscape and History in Central Italy*) remarks that except for marginal penetration 'the whole area between the coastal strip and the Tiber, for a distance of between fifty and sixty miles north-west of Rome, seems still to have been virtually untouched forest-land as late as 1000 BC'. (p. 7). Such forests continued to form a barrier to communications in South Etruria until with the construction of the Via Cassia in the latter half of the third century BC the area was laid open to Roman influence. One tract of forest land which evidently made a deep impression upon the Romans was the Silva Ciminia. Livy refers to its earlier reputation as follows: (Livy, IX, 36, 1): 'Silva erat Ciminia magis tum invia atque horrenda quam nuper fuere Germanici saltus, nulli ad eam diem ne mercatorum quidem adita. Eam intrare haud fere quisquam praeter ducem ipsum audebat'.

W. V. Harris (*Rome in Etruria and Umbria*, 1971, p. 55-6) considers that Livy's account contains 'some romantic elements, for example the description of the Ciminus itself'.[15] It is true that the Ciminian Forest like any other wild tract of land would be more difficult for those who did not know it or who were beset with enemies. Moreover it was not strictly able to be described as 'invia' if the Etruscans made any kind of road through it when going to Sutrium. But this raises the question of how much road-building the Etruscan army would have undertaken and what, if any, permanent effect it had on the terrain. It is probable that the area could still be described as 'invia atque horrenda' from the Roman point of view and from that of most other people unacquainted with it. 'Ducem' refers to a Roman leader and Livy's intention in the passage is clear from what he says in XXXVI, 6: 'sed neque commercium linguae nec vestis armorumque habitus sic eos texit, quam quod abhorrebat ab fide quemquam externum Ciminos saltus intraturum'. As for the merchants, they were unlikely to have chosen such a route, and the forest would remain 'invia' until Roman roads were made. Livy emphasises the difficult nature of the country by the use of the verb *penetrare* in XXXV, 3, and XXXVI, 6.

The Ciminian Forest, however, was only one of many, including those of Samnium, the Garganus and the Sila.[16] The Apennines themselves were forested and in some places covered with dense scrub of ilex and other evergreens.[17] Hannibal's efforts to cross the Apennines in winter are vividly described by Livy in XXI, 58. A few sentences will suffice to remind us of the conditions in that mountain area in the Spring of 217 BC as described by Livy:

'Transeuntem Appenninum adeo atrox adorta tempestas est ut Alpium prope foeditatem superaverit. Vento mixtus imber cum ferretur in ipsa ora, primo, quia aut arma omittenda erant aut contra enitentem vertice intorti adfligebantur, constitere . . . Et mox aqua levata vento cum super gelida montium iuga concreta esset, tantum nivosae grandinis deiecit ut omnibus omissis procumberent homines tegminibus suis magis obruti quam tecti . . . Multi homines, multa iumenta, elephanti quoque ex iis qui proelio ad Trebiam facto superfuerant septem absumpti.'

While some allowance may be made for exaggeration in this account, one must bear in mind that the first readers of this book might know something of the mountains and their climate, therefore an account too highly coloured would not have been acceptable. In fact if Livy's description of Hannibal's wanderings in Italy is studied as a whole it presents a fairly consistent picture. We are given an impression of the great contrasts between the fertile areas of intensive cultivation and the tracts of wild and almost impassable forests, mountains and marshes.

Further south travel was no easier, as may be seen from an earlier example. In 312 BC a Roman army was entering Apulia: 'eo consules cum valido exercitu venerunt: et primo circa saltus, cum utrimque ad hostem iniqua via esset, cunctati sunt'. The passages mentioned so far concern the third and fourth centuries BC. What of the early Empire, when the Roman road system in Italy was already well-developed and relations with the *socii* comparatively stable since the end of the Social War? Tacitus, in *Histories* III, 59, describes how the Flavian army crossed the Apennines in the winter:

'Sed foeda hieme per transitum Appennini conflictatus exercitus. Et vix quieto agmine nives eluctantibus patuit quantum discriminis adeundum foret, ni Vitellium retro fortuna vertisset.'

So it was still difficult — or had the 'Winter Crossing of the Apennines' become by this time a literary motif?

Although large areas of forest-land, especially in the uplands, were pathless in early Roman times, the Etruscans had their own local roads, often lined with tombs, leading from one of their cities to another. Judging by the influence of the Etruscans upon peoples to the east of the Apennines, such as those described by Cianfarani (*Antiche Civiltà d'Abruzzo*, 1969) it was possible for a pedlar on foot or muleback to travel across the peninsula to the Adriatic coast. To envisage any regular traffic across the Apennines at an early date would, however, involve the assumption that such trading contacts were always or usually direct, and not mediated through distant *emporia,* tribal gatherings or fairs. From Neolithic times shepherds and their flocks had moved between the mountains and the plains, but only at suitable seasons. For roads negotiable by wheeled traffic, crossing tribal boundaries and geographical barriers, we must wait until the end of the fourth century BC, and in many areas until much later. In the first century AD the by-road leading to the Younger Pliny's villa at Laurentum was difficult for carriages, and he advises (*Epist.* II, 17) that it should be traversed on horseback. Private roads were carefully protected, as in the inscription found near Citta-ducale in the Ager Cliterninus, now in the museum at L'Aquila: 'Via inferior privatast T. Umbreni C.f. Precario itur. Pecus, plostrum niquis agat.'[18] Even when the Roman roads were made, they did not necessarily help the local inhabitants to move from place to place. R. J. Buck writes of the Via Herculia: [19]

> 'It was not constructed with local needs in mind. The section from Potenza to Marsico Nuovo by-passes the inhabited areas of the Anzi and Platano valleys to strike through some rather desolate mountains'.

Other examples of the same kind are given in this article. In Central Italy the river valleys themselves had provided ancient routes from the coastal plains into the mountains and some of the rivers were navigable by small boats.[20] J. Le Gall (*Le Tibre dans l'Antiquité,* 1953, p. 18) refers to the navigation on the Tiber from Ripetta to Ponte Felice in 1905: 'on utilisait des chalands de 120 tonnes, longs de 35 m. sur 5 m. 80 de large'. Juvenal (*Sat.* VII, 121) writes of 'vinum Tiberi devectum'.

In considering communications as they affected peasant communities and occupiers of isolated farms, it should be remembered that they were not necessarily either so well equipped or of such strong physique as the members of military expeditions. Moreover if moving outside the boundaries of their own people they would, at any rate before the end of the Second Punic War, have encountered language difficulties. C. D. Buck[21] remarks that Oscan was used in official documents until the end of the Social War, 90-89 BC and that it continued to exist as a local dialect for some time after this. The Umbrian towns retained the use of their own language in inscriptions until 89 BC, though from the time of the Gracchi they adopted the Latin alphabet for this purpose.[22] The traveller was also an object of suspicion unless he could be clearly identified as a merchant or a shepherd. A countryman was often 'vicinae nescius urbis', as Claudian later describes him, and had therefore to be very self-sufficient in his day-to-day economy. Cato and Varro both stress the importance of this even on large estates.[23] It is still possible for a peasant in the uplands to be unacquainted with the nearest town, especially if that is not the place where he sells his produce. Even if it is, he will not usually stray beyond the market area and will leave as soon as his wares are sold and his purchases made.

Markets and fairs involving the exchange of produce and the sale of commodities not otherwise available to the countryman had existed at least since the Iron Age and exercised a considerable influence upon his style of living. Gierow (*The Iron Age Culture of Latium*, Vol. I, p. 423) writing of the work of the bronze smiths and other craftsmen in Latium says: 'The raw materials were not, however, available, but had to be acquired elsewhere, probably from craftsmen travelling from one village to another, or at the fairs which undoubtedly flourished, not least when religious festivals were celebrated or political meetings held. On these occasions it was certainly possible to acquire not only raw materials but also ready products . . .' Dionysius of Halicarnassus (III, 32) describes fairs and festivals at which countryfolk gathered, including one held in common by the Latins and Sabines.[24] The junction of two or more routes would have been a good site for a market, and MacMullen (*Market-Days in the Roman Empire, Phoenix*, 24 (1970) p. 333) refers to one in the Roman period:

'Such a site would stand no chance of mention in our written sources, and its tents and booths would leave little trace for the archaeologist; yet he might find at a cross-roads an area littered with coins, pottery, and other small objects attesting to the presence of crowds of people.'

Markets of this kind were very different from the well-organised *macellum* represented for example by the so-called 'Temple of

Serapis' at Pozzuoli. If we are to believe Apuleius, the efficiency
of Roman imperial government in this sphere was sometimes
laughable. In *Metamorphoses* I, 25, he recounts how Lucius
bought some fish in the market at Hypata, in Greece, for twenty
drachmae. The Market Inspector considered the price too high
and had the fish destroyed by his attendants. So Lucius lost his
money and his food. Much more like the *nundinae* as known to
the poorer country-dwellers was the market described by Petronius
(*Satyricon*, XV, 12, ed. Bücheler, pp. 13-14): 'veniebamus in
forum deficiente iam die, in quo notavimus frequentiam rerum
venalium, non quidem pretiosarum sed tamen quarum fidem male
ambulantem obscuritas temporis facillime tegeret.' The infor-
mality of the occasion is shown by the fact that Encolpius and
Ascyltus unroll the mantle in a dark corner and try to sell it,
without a stall or regular pitch — and yet they have some cus-
tomers. It is interesting to note that this market continued into
the evening: today this would be more likely to occur in the case
of an annual *festa* than a weekly market. Both types of gathering
existed in Roman Italy. Gabba[25] distinguishes between *nundinae*
which were held frequently and *mercatus* or *conventus*, annual
markets or fairs. He considers that the close connection of fairs
with religious cults often explains their survival into the medieval
period, since many pagan shrines and observances were put to
Christian use. In the first century AD *nundinae* were even held
on private estates, so that the landowner could dispose of his
surplus to his own tenants and staff: they likewise could sell to
each other on the same occasion. This reminds us of the difficulty
and expense involved in transporting goods by land in ancient
Italy. It was greatly to the advantage of the farmer to dispose
of his produce locally.

In many parts of Italy, and in the islands, one may still find
conditions of agricultural work and local communications almost
unaltered since Roman times or even earlier. Moreover we are
fortunate in possessing detailed information regarding particular
areas of Italy, where the nature of the terrain and the small scale
of the land-holdings invite comparison with those known to
peasant farmers in the Roman period. One such area is to be

found at Borgo a Mozzano, twenty-one miles from Lucca in Tuscany, where an agricultural experiment conducted under the auspices of Shell Italiana from 1954-1961 has been carefully documented.[26] Borgo a Mozzano covers an area in the Apennines of 6,689 hectares, of which more than 60 per cent is woodland. It contains sixteen hamlets, six in the mountains, five in hill-country, and five in the valley of the river Serchio. Nine of these hamlets could until 1954 be reached only by mule-track. Goods had to be carried up from the main village by mules or men, and this involved two or three hours of rough walking (Virone, *Borgo a Mozzano*, p. 18). There were in 1963 3,745 land-holdings in the comune of Borgo a Mozzano and their average area was 1.69 hectares.[27] These holdings were usually grouped together, producing an average farm of 3.83 hectares. In 1961 the inhabitants of this area gave 11, 252 working days to road-making in order to improve their communications with the world outside. Such efforts, which were made voluntarily, are a sufficient indication of the inconvenience and disadvantage which they had experienced through the years. Borgo a Mozzano was not unusual, in fact it was chosen for this experiment as a typical area of small-scale farming with low productivity on marginal land.

The conditions in which the small farmer in the upland regions of Italy lived and worked in the Roman period must have borne a very close resemblance to those of Borgo a Mozzano as it was until 1954. Although the number of small farms was subject to important variations in course of time, if we consider the whole period from 500 BC to the end of the second century AD, small-scale agriculture must be regarded as one of the main occupations pursued in Italy. The level of culture, technical achievement and quality of life attainable in such a way depended to a large extent upon the accessibility of neighbours, markets and urban centres. The large number of markets, daily, weekly or seasonal, which are still held in Italy throw some light upon the ancient situation. From the map provided by Nice in the *Rivista geografica*[28] and reproduced on page 30 we can study the distribution of markets in Tuscany in the twentieth century. The present siting of these markets has been influenced by medieval conditions

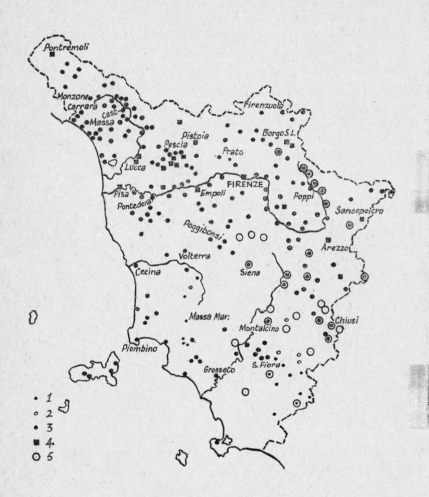

2. Map of Tuscany showing markets in 1953,
from: 'Per uno studio geografico dei mercati periodici della Toscana',
in Rivista geografica italiana, Vol. 62 (1955), Florence, p. 311.

    1. Markets held monthly.
    2. Markets held fortnightly.
    3. Weekly markets.
    4. Markets held more than once a week.
    5. Fairs held monthly.

4. Small-scale cultivation at Villalago (L'Aquila).

3. The Apennine barrier.

found at Borgo a Mozzano, twenty-one miles from Lucca in Tuscany, where an agricultural experiment conducted under the auspices of Shell Italiana from 1954-1961 has been carefully documented.[26] Borgo a Mozzano covers an area in the Apennines of 6,689 hectares, of which more than 60 per cent is woodland. It contains sixteen hamlets, six in the mountains, five in hill-country, and five in the valley of the river Serchio. Nine of these hamlets could until 1954 be reached only by mule-track. Goods had to be carried up from the main village by mules or men, and this involved two or three hours of rough walking (Virone, *Borgo a Mozzano*, p. 18). There were in 1963 3,745 land-holdings in the comune of Borgo a Mozzano and their average area was 1.69 hectares.[27] These holdings were usually grouped together, producing an average farm of 3.83 hectares. In 1961 the inhabitants of this area gave 11, 252 working days to road-making in order to improve their communications with the world outside. Such efforts, which were made voluntarily, are a sufficient indication of the inconvenience and disadvantage which they had experienced through the years. Borgo a Mozzano was not unusual, in fact it was chosen for this experiment as a typical area of small-scale farming with low productivity on marginal land.

The conditions in which the small farmer in the upland regions of Italy lived and worked in the Roman period must have borne a very close resemblance to those of Borgo a Mozzano as it was until 1954. Although the number of small farms was subject to important variations in course of time, if we consider the whole period from 500 BC to the end of the second century AD, small-scale agriculture must be regarded as one of the main occupations pursued in Italy. The level of culture, technical achievement and quality of life attainable in such a way depended to a large extent upon the accessibility of neighbours, markets and urban centres. The large number of markets, daily, weekly or seasonal, which are still held in Italy throw some light upon the ancient situation. From the map provided by Nice in the *Rivista geografica*[28] and reproduced on page 30 we can study the distribution of markets in Tuscany in the twentieth century. The present siting of these markets has been influenced by medieval conditions

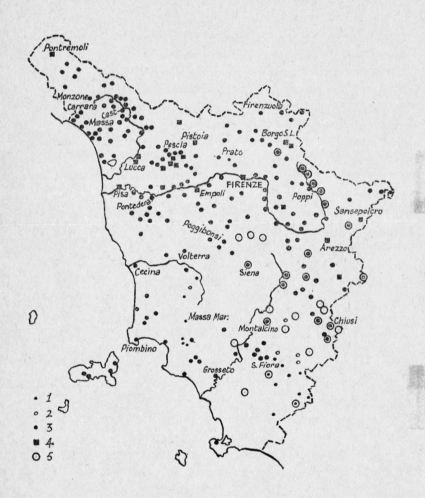

2. Map of Tuscany showing markets in 1953,
from: '*Per uno studio geografico dei mercati periodici della Toscana*',
in Rivista geografica italiana, Vol. 62 (1955), Florence, p. 311.

1. Markets held monthly.
2. Markets held fortnightly.
3. Weekly markets.
4. Markets held more than once a week.
5. Fairs held monthly.

as well as those of the Roman period. Nice emphasises the effect of geographical and economic factors in determining the position of the markets, but adds (p. 315) that tradition has played a large part also. For our purpose it is the number of these markets and their position in relation to geographical features and to their catchment areas that is important. The main concentrations of weekly markets can be found in the valleys of the Serchio and the Arno, extending the whole length of the rivers, up into the Apuan Alps and the Apennines respectively. Other significant features are the three centres on the lower reaches of the Magra, covering the part of its course which was navigable in ancient times. Between the Magra and the Serchio they follow the Via Aurelia. The valley of the Umbro has its share of market sites, and outside the river valleys those in the neighbourhood of the Via Cassia are conspicuous. The isolation experienced by the countryman in ancient Italy was not always that of an individual farm, but of a very small community relying almost entirely upon its own resources.[29] Without access to regular markets and where there was only a single holding, the cultivator would have to be his own blacksmith, builder and supplier of plants and seeds, as well as of remedies for the ailments of man and beast. Where there were more farmsteads, some differentiation of function could take place, but still within narrow limits.

Notes to Chapter One

1. A. N. Sherwin-White, *The Roman Citizenship*, 1939, p. 8; M. Pallottino in *Civiltà del Lazio primitivo*, 1976, p. 41.
2. Dion. Hal. III, 32; Strabo, V, 2, 9.
3. A. Alföldi, *Early Rome and the Latins*, 1963, p. 3; R. M. Ogilvie, *Commentary on Livy I-V*, 1965, p. 665.
4. cf. Strabo, V, 3, 2.
5. He is touching here upon the disappearance or assimilation of some of the smaller tribes in the sub-Apennine districts.
6. W. F. Jashemski, *The Discovery of a Market-garden Orchard at Pompeii*, American Journal of Archaeology, vol. 79, 1974, pp. 391-404.

7. This was where Vettidius held his meagre celebrations, Persius, *Satires* IV, 28.

8. cf. Virgil, *Georgics* II, 382.

9. Livy, XXV, 5, 6; XXXIX, 14, 7; XL, 37, 1; XLIII, 14, 10.

10. Sherwin-White, op. cit., pp. 74-5, shows that some *conciliabula* acquired a certain amount of local organisation.

11. *Civil War and Society in Southern Etruria* in *War and Society*, ed. M. R. D. Foot, 1975, p. 279; *Capena and the Ager Capenas*, PBSR, 1962, p. 126. Archaeological evidence for settlement patterns in another part of Italy should soon be available from the Molise Project (Graeme Barker).

12. Strabo, V. 3, 1, of the Sabine: 'πόλεις δ'ἔχουσιν ὀλίγας καὶ τεταπεινωμένας διὰ τοὺς συνεχεῖς πολέμους - - - -';of the tribes in the Central Apennines (V, 4, 2); 'τὰ μὲν οὖν ἄλλα κωμηδὸν ζῶσιν, ἔχουσι δὲ καὶ πόλεις - - - - -'

13. Livy XXXI, 26, 10, used with reference to village comunities in Attica.

14. cf. Virgil, *Aeneid* VII, 601 to end, where the description of the 'gathering of the clans' relies upon this regionalism for its appeal.

15. But for another account, which stresses the importance of forest barriers in this area, see G. Duncan, *Sutri (Sutrium)* in PBSR, XIII (1958) p. 77ff.

16. Also in Lucania. See E. Magaldi, *Lucania Romana*, p. 47: 'Nell' antichità il bosco in Lucania era molto più esteso di quanto non sia oggi. Al principio del secolo scorso il mantello boschivo ricopriva ancora un terzo della regione'.

17. Virgil refers to this in *Aeneid* XII, 701-2.

18. Degrassi, ILLR, no. 489, p. 282.

19. PBSR, XXIX, 1971, p. 86.

20. As for example the Anio, the Nar and the Teneas (Strabo, V, 2, 10, and V, 3, 7). See also Pliny, *N.H.* III, 5 (54) and Livy II, 34, and R. M. Ogilvie's note on the passage.

21. *A Grammar of Oscan and Umbrian*, New York, 1974, pp. 4-5. On the language problem in Italy before the Social War, see also P. A. Brunt, *Italian Aims at the Time of the Social War*, JRS, LV (1965) pp. 98-9.

22. J. Heurgon, *L'Ombrie à l'Epoque des Gracques et de Sylla*, in *Problemi di Storia e Archeologia dell 'Umbria*, 1964, pp. 113-114.

23. For the suggestion that this attitude was a legacy from earlier times, see K. D. White, *Roman Farming*, p. 51.

24. cf. IV, 49, the festival of Jupiter Latiaris.

25. In *Mercati e Fiere nell'Italia romana*, *Studi classici e orientali*, XXIV, 1975. For a list of fairs connected with shrines, see pp. 155-6 of the same article.

26. *Borgo a Mozzano* by L. E. Virone, World Land Use Survey, Occasional Papers, no. 4, Bude, 1963.
27. The comparable figure given by Virone for Italy as a whole in 1963 was 2.87 hectares.
28. Bruno Nice, *Per uno studio geografico dei mercati periodici della Toscana*, in *Rivista geografica italiana*, vol. 62 (1955), p. 311.
29. For such a community in the nineteenth century, and lists of the occupations of its inhabitants, see L. Grottanelli, *La Maremma toscana*, I, *Roccastrada*. Siena, 1873. This situation must have been paralleled in many small Roman settlements.

CHAPTER TWO

Pastoralism

In our ancient sources pastoralism is accorded even more importance than agriculture as the occupation of the earliest inhabitants
of Rome itself — 'illa pastorum convenarumque plebs'. (Livy II,
1, 3.)[1] Livy, foreshortening a long process in the interests of
rhetoric, makes Camillus say (V, 53, 9): 'Maiores nostri, convenae
pastoresque, cum in his locis nihil praeter silvas paludesque esset,
novam urbem tam brevi aedificarunt . . .' Varro (*Res Rusticae* II,
9) asks: 'Romanorum vero populum a pastoribus esse ortum quis
non dicit?' In Virgil, *Aeneid* VII, 406ff, the people of Latium ruled
by Latinus and Turnus are described as *pastores* and *agrestes*
(once only as *agricolae*, line 521) while the incomers, the Trojans,
perhaps significantly are *coloni* (line 422). The Fury rousing them
to war 'pastorale signum canit'. After the first conflict:

'ruit omnis in urbem
pastorum ex acie numerus'. (573-4).

Pastor may denote a herdsman of any kind, not necesarily a
shepherd, for which the special word *opilio* was available. Varro
often uses *pastor* for a herdsman in charge of cattle or goats.[2] In
Res Rusticae II, 11-12, he uses the expression *scientia pastoralis*
for all types of animal husbandry, including the keeping of sheep,

goats, pigs, oxen and horses. The herdsmen who are needed to tend these animals are all *pastores* (II, 12). The idea of shepherd villages or towns, that is communities where most if not all the male inhabitants were shepherds is interesting.[3] This still occurs at the present day when, for example, in the district of Nuoro in Sardinia, Oliena and Fonni are shepherd villages, while Bitti is a cattle-raising and dairy-farming village. It is possible that such a distinction between communities existed on the mainland of Italy in the Roman period. This situation may sometimes result from the practice of transhumance in a particular area. If, as E. H. Carrier (*Water and Grass*, London, 1932) suggested, the Romans and the Sabines had reciprocal pasturage arrangements in the sixth or seventh century BC, this would have assisted the early development of Rome as a shepherd village. It seems likely, however, that at a very early stage the Roman citizen had his *hortus* and that agriculture was associated with pastoralism. Virgil probably describes the usual custom in Central Italy when he writes in *Aeneid* XI, 318-9:

'Aurunci Rutulique serunt, et vomere duros
exercent collis atque horum asperrima pascunt'.

There are three processes here: the Aurunci and Rutuli plant their kitchen-gardens on whatever level ground there is, they plough the gentler slopes of the hills, and they pasture sheep and goats on the rugged heights.

The Romans attributed a certain remoteness, perhaps also a roughness and lack of culture, to the herdsmen.[4] To some extent this arose from the wildness and loneliness of the pastures:

'per loca pastorum deserta atque otia dia'. (Lucretius,
De Rerum Natura, V, 1389.)

Their strangeness must have been increased where transhumance was practised, for this involved separation for several months from their native villages. Although the herdsmen could be accompanied by their womenfolk, this migration inevitably divided them from the other inhabitants of the countryside. Braudel (*The Mediterranean*, vol. I, p. 85) regards transhumance as a relic of nomadism, and, if this is so, some early shepherd communities may have represented a more primitive culture than that of the settled tribes surrounding them. Some of the shepherds' activities must have seemed inimical to the interests of the farmers. Shepherds in Apulia, we are told, burned off the vegetation so that flocks could browse on the fresh shoots.[5] Virgil (*Georgics* II, 303) refers to shepherds accidentally causing forest fires:

'nam saepe incautis pastoribus excidit ignis'.

Is this really part of the same process?[6] Pliny (*N.H.* XVI, 77 (208)) describes the ways in which *pastores* and *exploratores* make fires. Braudel distinguishes two kinds of transhumance, normal (from plains to mountains) and inverse, where people domiciled in mountain areas descend to the plains in winter with their flocks. The Younger Pliny (*Epist.* II, 17, 3) describes the inverse movement of flocks in writing of the neighbourhood of his villa at Laurentum: 'multi greges ovium, multa ibi equorum boum armenta, quae montibus hieme depulsa herbis et tepore verno nitescunt'. This passage reminds us that sheep were not the only animals moved annually to pasturage in this way. The practice has continued up to the present day, and in 1953 a million sheep were involved, of which 33,000 in Tuscany were transported to their new pastures by rail.[7] These figures give some idea of the importance of this annual migration.

Transhumant flocks in ancient Italy followed the drove-roads which are known as *calles* in Latin, and *tratturi* in modern Italian. The summer *saltus* or pastures were the higher grasslands, such as the mountain slopes in Umbria, the Abruzzi, Campania and Calabria (E. H. Carrier, *Water and Grass,* p. 38). These areas included large expanses of wild country where shepherds and their flocks wandered freely. In the late Republic and the Empire, however, the grazing was controlled as far as was practicable, and pasture grounds were rented from the state. Most of the winter pasturage on the plains was privately owned or belonged to a particular community. In 111 BC free pasturage was granted to all flocks on the march by the Agrarian Law in the following terms:

'If anyone brings flocks onto the drove-roads or public highways for the purpose of travel and there pastures them, he shall not be liable to pay anything to the community or to the tax collector in respect of those beasts which he has pastured on the drove-roads or public highways, having driven them there for the purpose of travel.'[8]

This was only one of the problems raised by the large-scale movement of livestock in a country where the population far exceeded the level appropriate to nomadic activities, and all were subject to the rule of law. Damage might be caused by stray animals, herdsmen might halt their flocks in unauthorised places, quarrel among themselves or turn to brigandage.[9] A *scriptura censoria* was levied on all flocks using the *calles*, to pay for the upkeep and policing of the routes. Tacitus (*Annals* IV, 27, 2) mentions a quaestor who was in charge of the drove-roads. In the fifteenth and sixteenth centuries the task of supervising the movement of the flocks fell to the *Dogana delle Pecore*. In Puglia in the fifteenth century arrangements were made by which farmers had the use of pasture when the shepherds left it.[10] It may have been possible to utilise such land in ancient Italy before the growth of large estates and the spread of more intensive farming methods led to the imposition of legal controls.

These drove-roads, which already existed in prehistoric times, perhaps as early as the Bronze Age, were wide, unpaved tracks.[11] Taking advantage of natural features of the landscape the main *calles* offered easily distinguishable routes to the high Apennines for the transhumant flocks and their herdsmen. They are marked today by the line of towns or villages which owe their origin to the migration of the flocks. These may be compared to the villages in Scotland which have grown up in places where the shielings were built on the summer pastures (E. C. Curwen, *Plough and Pasture*, p. 82). On one route were Bovianum, Saepinum and Beneventum.[12] The enlargement of some of the settlements into towns may belong rather to the medieval than to the Roman period, but their earlier importance to the herdsmen and their camp-followers can hardly be in doubt. Larinum stood at the meeting place of several routes and provided a market for livestock. Luceria was a centre of the wool trade. Capracotta, the highest town in peninsular Italy (1416 m.) was also on the path of the transhumant flocks. Between Capracotta and Agnone was found the Agnone Tablet, which lists in Oscan the agricultural deities of the neighbourhood and can be dated c. 250 BC.[13] The seventeen rustic deities named seem to be agricultural rather than pastoral, though it may be significant that Hercules is among them. The existence of certain religious cults among shepherd communities chiefly or exclusively is an indication of the distinctiveness of the pastoral way of life. F. van Wonterghem (*L'Antiquité classique,* vol. XLII, 1, 1973, 36-48) has traced in detail the worship of Hercules among the Paeligni and concludes that it was connected with the transhumant shepherds. Traces of shrines and figurines have been found along the *tratturi.*[14] These discoveries relate to the end of the third century BC and the beginning of the second. Better known pastoral deities are Pales and Silvanus. Pales is celebrated by the poets as the god of shepherds:

'hinc ego pastoremque meum lustrare quot annis
et placidam soleo spargere lacte Palem'.

Tibullus I, 35-6; cf II, 5, 28-32.

The Palilia or shepherds' festival in honour of Pales was held at the beginning of spring, and sacrifices were offered in thanksgiving for the increase of the flocks.[15]

Even in areas subject to extremes of climate the practice of transhumance was not universal in historical times. The small farmer was less likely to embark upon the long journey to summer pastures than the owner of large flocks.[16] On a mixed farm it was possible to feed and house a small flock of sheep throughout the winter in most districts. Tradition played a major part in deciding the method of husbandry adopted in each locality. Most of the information about sheep-farming which we find in the works of the agronomists concerns the large-scale operations of wealthy land-owners or the activities of their employees, whether slave or free. However, as Philenium says to Cleaereta in Plautus, *Asinaria* (lines 540-1):

'etiam opilio qui pascit, mater, alienas oves,
aliquam habet peculiarem qui spem soletur suam'.

K. D. White (op. cit., p. 399) lists the products of a sheep-station on a large estate as wool, hides, meat and cheese, in that order of importance. This is one respect in which the activities of the small and large farms differed. It is unlikely that the production of wool was of first importance to the farmer at subsistence level. He could have sold some of it, if he was in a locality from which he could transport it to the appropriate markets, but these might be a considerable distance away. Both the quantity and the quality of the smallholder's product would often make it unsatisfactory for commercial use. Columella (VII, 3, 9) emphasises the importance of pasturing sheep on grassland which is free from thorns, and he includes the two lines of Virgil, *Georgics* III, 384-5:

'Si tibi lanitium curae est, primum aspera silva
lappaeque tribulique absint.'

The poorer the farmer, the less likely he would be to have a choice of pasture and to be able to use land of good quality for this purpose. On the other hand let us suppose that he used the wool himself or sold it locally. If Cato's slaves only had a new tunic every two years,[17] the poorer countryfolk probably did not have one much more frequently. The provision Cato advises for the workers on an estate is intended to be adequate, and indeed is sometimes generous, as for example in the supply of hoods for some workers (Cato X, 5, and XI, 5). The peasant farmer working to supply his own and his family's requirements would not have needed a great amount of wool.

It seems likely that in ancient Italy the use of milk for cheese was more important to the small farmer than either meat or wool production. Writing of the sheep, Columella (VII, 2, 1) says: 'Tum etiam casei lactisque abundantia non solum agrestes saturat, sed etiam elegantium mensas iucundis et numerosis dapibus exornat'. Meat was not a staple article of diet for any except the rich in the Roman period. Where the peasant is depicted as consuming any meat at all, it is usually bacon or pork, smoked in the *carnarium*. The one purpose for which the smallholder in the uplands might sell a sheep or slaughter it himself would be for a sacrifice upon some religious festival. While we

should not underestimate the incidence of such celebrations in
the villages and the *pagi* or on the individual farm (as in Tibullus
I, 1, 22) they were by their very nature interruptions of a routine
which must have been chiefly directed to other ends.

The smallholder who kept sheep or goats must have done so
mainly for the milk products they supplied. It is the duty of the
shepherd to make cheese, says Columella (XII, 13). This refers
to the shepherd employed on the large estate, but the custom
has its origin in a practical necessity. The cheese was easier to
transport than the liquid milk, which would quickly deteriorate
in hot weather. Since a particular vessel, known as *mulctra* òr
mulctrum, was used as a milking-pail, what could be simpler
than to curdle the milk in the pail and turn it into curd cheese
on the spot? The *mulctra* is thought by K. D. White (*Farm Equipment of the Roman World*, p. 171) to have been a round, fairly
shallow bowl made of earthenware. If it was earthenware, and not
composed either wholly or partly of metal, it would have to be
low and firmly-based, or it would have been easily knocked over
by the animal. It is interesting to note that Latin has this special
word for a milking-vessel. In Greek πέλλα can be used for
this, but it is often just an ἀγγεῖον. In a note to Theocritus I,
26, Cholmeley points out in his edition of 1901 that 'ἐς δύο
πέλλας' means 'as much as two pails full' (so A. S. F. Gow,
Theocritus, Vol. II, p. 6, 1950) and not 'into two pails'. The
practical implication of this phrase is that the πέλλα used
for milking must have been of a standard size, intended to contain
the normal yield of one animal. The *mulctra* may also have been
so designed. The Scythians (Herodotus, IV, 2) collected milk into
a large vat or barrel — but this is recounted by Herodotus as
one of the strange and barbaric features of their milking arrangements. It seems unlikely that on the small farm milk was accumu-
lated in large containers. It will not keep; it must be transported
if it is to be sold; and vessels of this kind would be very difficult
to clean. The making of curd cheese in such large vessels would
seem to involve considerable difficulties, at any rate for a man
working on his own. What happened to the milk after it reached
the pail is described by Homer in a simile in Iliad XVI, 641-3:

'As when at spring-tide the cattle-sheds
Around the milk-cans swarm the buzzing flies,
While the warm milk is frothing in the pail.'

Lord Derby, translating this in 1864, wrote in the terms of his own day of 'cattle-sheds' and 'milk-cans'. 'Cattle' are not specified in the Greek, and the 'milk-can' is a πέλλα. The question as to whether the ancient Romans and Italians used chiefly sheep's milk or cow's milk, and which they preferred, is somewhat otiose. In many parts of Southern and Central Italy suitable grazing for cows did not exist and therefore, if milk was required, it had to be obtained from sheep or goats. Literary references suggest that sheep's milk was very frequently used for cheese-making.

Two main types of cheese were made in ancient Italy, the curd or cottage cheese, which is simple to make but must be eaten fresh, and the hard, long-lasting cheese, which could be stored by the householder and carried as rations by shepherds and travellers. The curd cheese was what the Cyclops, Polyphemus, made, as described in *Odyssey* IX, 244. He sat down and milked his sheep and goats, then put the young under their mothers again. Immediately after this (αὐτίκα) he curdled half the milk and put it in wicker baskets. The rest he placed 'ἐν ἄγγεσιν', for drinking. Neither the Greeks nor the Romans were keen milk-drinkers, and it may well be as a further touch of savagery that the Cyclops is thus depicted.[18] It is the duty of the shepherd not only to make cheese but to take it to the market and sell it (Virgil, *Ecl.* I, 33-5). The milk obtained during the evening must be made into cheese and put into frails to drain.[19] Then it is sold the next morning — 'adit oppida pastor' — that is, the shepherd goes to town himself. All this happens because the cheese would not remain fresh and it must be sold promptly before it dries too much.

The method of making the hard cheese is described by Palladius, VI, 9, 'de caseo faciendo', as one of the activities of the month of May. The full-cream (sincero) milk is to be curdled with rennet obtained from a lamb or goat,[20] or with a piece of membrane taken from the stomach of a chicken. The flowers of the wild thistle or the juice of the fig can also be used. The mention of

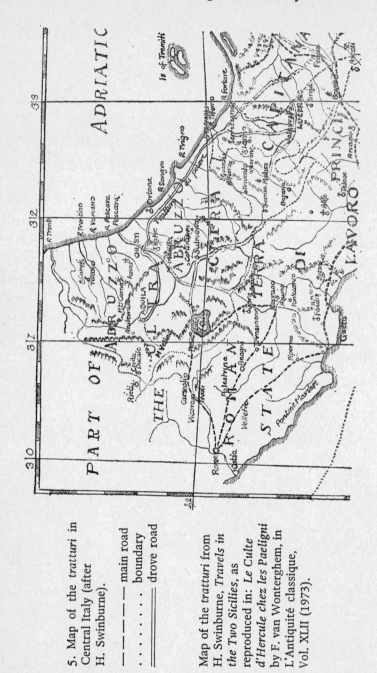

5. Map of the *tratturi* in Central Italy (after H. Swinburne).

------- main road

.... boundary

════════ drove road

Map of the *tratturi* from H. Swinburne, *Travels in the Two Sicilies*, as reproduced in: *Le Culte d'Hercule chez les Paeligni* by F. van Wonterghem, in L'Antiquité classique, Vol. XLII (1973).

several alternatives here (cf. Col. VII, 8, 1) suggests that they were originally local expedients adopted by the peasant farmer. Rennet was made from the 'beestings', that is the first milk given by an animal after producing its offspring (Latin: *colostrum, coagulum;* Greek: πυετία). Only a small amount of rennet was required — according to Columella (VII, 8, 2) the weight of a silver *denarius.* After mentioning the means of curdling the milk, Palladius continues:

'ubi solidari coeperit, loco opaco ponatur aut frigido et pressus subinde adiectis pro adquisita soliditate ponderibus, trito ac torrefacto sale debet aspergi et iam durior vehementius premi'.

After a few days when the moulded cheeses have set, they are to be laid out on hurdles so that they do not touch each other. They are thus to be dried, under cover, away from the wind so that they do not become tough. Such cheeses would form a useful addition to the countryman's diet, especially in mountainous areas where olives were not available as a relish and a source of nourishment. It is noticeable that Cato does not suggest cheese as a ration for the slaves on the type of farm he is discussing. They are to have bread, olives, fish sauce, vinegar, oil and salt (Cato LVI-LVIII). This presupposes a farm in an olive-growing district with access to commercial sources for condiments.

The works of the agronomists contain many more details on the subject of animal husbandry, but only occasionally is it possible to detect among them expedients derived from small-scale farming or methods which are only applicable to the small-holding. Traditional ways of handling and housing farm animals, as well as of curing their diseases, are recommended by writers of the early Empire to contemporary landowners and doubtless were used by them or by their workers. But what of Virgil? Have we neglected the *Eclogues,* which should be particularly important for the subject of this chapter? The picture of the shepherd which we obtain from these poems is not always easy to interpret in terms of the activities of herdsmen in Italy at the time when they were written. The influence of the Hellenistic tradition of pastoral poetry tends to obscure the practicalities and, as in *Georgics* III, we are often transported to a Greek or Eastern

Mediterranean environment. Such pastorals, however, owe their very existence to the impression of remoteness which shepherds gave to the plainsman and the town-dweller. Moreover amid all their literary embellishments the *Eclogues* portray the herdsman facing the real problems of his calling. Meliboeus reminds us of the difficulty of dealing with animals which give birth to their young during migration or transhumance (I, 13-15 and 49-50). There is the intense heat of the pastures in summer (II, 8-13 and III, 98-9): even the meadows have to be irrigated (III, 111). Moeris' farm is occupied by a new *colonus* (IX, 2-4). As pastoral poems the *Eclogues* focus attention upon countrymen as shepherds. Yet in Eclogue I Tityrus keeps cattle and sheep, makes cheese and sells it, and is able to offer apples and chestnuts by way of hospitality. Meliboeus keeps goats, grows corn, pears and vines. These men belong neither to the ranch nor to the semi-nomadic shepherd village. They are the peasant proprietors of small, mixed farms, who tend their own flocks, still a familiar feature of the countryside which Virgil knew.

Notes to Chapter Two

1. 'Pastorum convenarumque' seems almost a hendiadys here, shepherds being regarded as outlanders by the settled plainsman.
2. cf Ovid, *Fasti*, 879.
3. For the existence of this type of community in the medieval period, see, for example, Benedetto Croce, *Storia del Regno di Napoli*, p. 340. Of Pescasseroli in the Abruzzo he writes: 'La populazione si componeva quasi tutta di pastori'. On p. 355 he notes that at a later date (1658) there were in this town 665 inhabitants, mostly 'pecorali', with a few 'aratori' or 'braccianti'. There were also a small number of 'bassettieri', that is, dealers in the skins of stillborn lambs (bassette).
4. As in the incident described by Livy in X, 4, 4. cf G. W. W. Barker, *Prehistoric Territories and Economies in Central Italy*, in *Palaeoeconomy*, ed. E. S. Higgs, p. 156; 'Perhaps the beginnings of this social dichotomy can be found in the later Bronze Age, as lowland and upland settlements developed in the latter part of the second millenium BC: there is a striking difference between the assemblages of poor coarse wares in the Faliscan caves and shelters on the trans-

humant route to the Maremma and those of the contemporaneous levels at the Narce settlement, less than 20 km to the south.'

5. Lucan, *Pharsalia* IX, 182-5; Silius, *Punica* VII, 364-6; Virgil, *Georgics* II, 303.

6. For the burning of woodland in ancient Liguria, see Sereni, *Comunità rurali nell 'Italia antica*, p. 539.

7. G. Barbieri, 'Osservazioni geografico — statistiche sulla transumanza in Italia', in *Rivista geografica italiana*, Vol. 62, 1955.

8. For the Latin text see CIL IX, 2438, and E. H. Warmington, ROL, IV, p. 392. U. Laffi (*L'Iscrizione di Sepino* in *Studi classici e orientali* XIV (1965), p. 188) thinks that this inscription shows that the use of the *calles* was free in the time of the Republic. This it would seem to do, unless any distinction is to be made between driving flocks along the *calles* and allowing them to graze at certain points on the way. In the fifteenth century there were pastures set aside for this purpose along the transhumance routes. Dora Musto (*La Regia Dogana della mena delle pecore di Puglia*, p. 25, note 7) writes of these: 'I tratturi si dipartivano dall'Aquila, da Celano e da Pescasseroli e con percorsi diversi convergano tutti in Foggia. A fianco di essi erano situati vari 'riposti laterali' ossia pascoli in cui sostavano le greggi lungo il cammino'.

9. Livy XXXIX, 29, 4 (these shepherds were slaves from large estates). Pliny, *Epist.* VI, 25 — a kidnapping incident in Umbria. Pliny does not mention shepherds but it is in sheep-rearing country; Strabo, IV, 6, 9 and VI, 2, 6.

10. D. Musto, *La Regia Dogana*, p. 18: '. . . dal 29 settembre all' 8 maggio di ogni anno le erbe censite dal fisco venivano cedute ai pastori, per tornare nel resto dell'anno ai legittimi propietari che potevano liberamente disporre del pascolo estivo.'

11. E. T. Salmon, *Samnium and the Samnites*, p. 69, states that a typical drovers' trail was over a hundred yards wide. In *L'Archivio del Tavoliere di Puglia*, ed. P. Di Cicco and D. Musto, p. 121, there is a seventeenth-century map of a *tratturo* which has a road running through it. Measurements of the ground on each side of the road are shown, to indicate the total width of the official sheep track.

12. For a map showing the routes of modern transhumance throughout Europe, see Braudel, op. cit., p. 98. G. Colonna (*Saepinum: Ricerche di Topografia sannitica e medioevale, Archeologia classica*, XIV (1962) 80-107) writes of a 'Porta del Tratturo' at Saepinum — the gate leading directly from the ancient town to the drove-road.

13. *Grammatik der Oskisch-Umbrischen Dialekte*, Vol. II, R. von Planta, no. 200; *Italic Dialects*, R. S. Conway, no. 175.

14. A map of the tratturi, after H. Swinburne, *Travels in the Two*

Sicilies, Vol. I (reproduced from that of F. van Wonterghem, op. cit., fig. 12) appears on page 42.

15. Dion, Hal. I, 883; Ovid, Fasti IV, 721ff; Tibullus II, 5, 87-8.

16. An example of this in the twentieth century can be found in Marie Mauron's account (*La Transhumance du Pays d'Arles aux grandes Alpes*, Part I) of her stay with a shepherd family from La Crau d'Arles who were travelling to the high Alps with their flocks. They took with them additional sheep from some smaller farms in the neighbourhood. This function was performed by the *conductores* in the Roman period, and Laffi (*L'Iscrizione di Sepino*, p. 184) discusses whether they had to return to the owners only the number of sheep received from them, or the lambs also. They presumably had the use of the products of the flock, such as cheese and wool, for themselves.

17. Cato, *De Agri Cultura*, LIX.

18. As in the case of the Getae, Col. VII, 2, 2.

19. For a description of such cheese-making in the nineteenth century, see George Dennis, *Cities and Cemeteries of Etruria*, Vol. I (1907 edition) p. 99: 'Though a fierce May sun blazed without, a huge fire roared in the middle of the hut; but this was for the sake of the *ricotta*, which was being made in another part of the *capanna*. Here stood a huge cauldron, full of boiling ewes' milk . . . Lord of the cauldron, stood a man dispensing ladlefuls of the rich simmering mess to his fellows, as they brought their bowls for their morning's allowance; and he varied his occupation by pouring the same into certain small baskets, the serous parts running off through the wicker, and the residue caking as it cooled. On the same board stood the cheeses, previously made from the cream.'

20. Varro, *R.R.* II, 11, 4, says that rennet is better from a hare or a kid than from a lamb.

CHAPTER THREE

The Year's Work on the Small Farm

In considering the work of the smallholder on the farmstead we may begin by studying the schedules available to us from the Roman period, some of which are literary, some in the form of inscriptions and some pictorial. Varro, Virgil and Columella all include in the course of their works a series of farming activities arranged according to the seasons, or in the case of Columella, the months of the year. Palladius makes such a calendar the basis of his *Opus Agriculturae*, Books II-XIII having the names of the months. It is desirable, however, to set beside these the non-literary evidence provided by the *Menologia Rustica* and the pictorial examples such as the mosaic from St. Romain en Gal,[1] and the illustrations accompanying the calendar recently discovered beneath the church of S. Maria Maggiore in Rome. Such displays of information are far more likely to have been glimpsed by the farming community than are the works of the literary élite. Though the *menologia* in the form in which they are known today, that is the *Colotianum* and the *Vallense*,[2] are probably not earlier than the first century AD, there is some reason to suppose that they are the products of a long tradition. They are based upon a pre-Julian calendar, which Mommsen (*Römische Chronologie*, Berlin, 1859, p. 56) shows to have been connected with that of Eudoxus, and to have avoided the use of the intercalary month which caused such difficulties to farmers.[3] These *menologia* are thought to belong to the suburban area near Rome,[4] though some have considered that the mention (Mensis Martius, in *Colotianum*, Degrassi, p. 287) of *trimestre* being sown implies that the calendar derives from a cold climate, perhaps in an upland region. *Trimestre* or three-month wheat is described by Pliny, *N.H.* XVIII, 12 (69) as being particularly suitable for regions with a cold climate, but Columella (II, 98) takes him to task for this and asserts that there is no seed which by nature requires only three months to grow. Even *trimestre* will do better, he says, if planted in the autumn and given longer to come to fruition.

The activities described in the *menologia* are the most basic to the existence of the small farmer engaged in mixed husbandry; they include the main stages of grain and pulse production, harvest, vintage, fruit-picking, olive-gathering. Less important items, as it might seem to us, but nevertheless considered worthy of a place in these inscriptions, are the cutting of reeds and the waterproofing of *dolia*.[5] The reeds formed the material for shelters, mats and baskets, and the *dolia* had to be proofed for the storage of wine and many kinds of food and drink. Covering these and other vessels with pitch was a task which had to be completed by the time of the vintage and of the harvesting of the various types of produce: a reminder in the calendar would be helpful. The language of the *Colotianum* has some peculiarities thought to be colloquialisms, such as 'aquitur' for 'acuitur' (January) and the use of present participles where finite verbs might be expected, as in 'fabam serentes, materias deicientes' (December). These inscriptions differ in style from the writings of the agronomists especially in this use of participles, and because they do not use the imperative at all, thus indicating that their purpose is somewhat different from that of their literary counterparts. The *Menologia* contain mere jottings of the operations which could be timed with some exactitude and assigned to a particular month.

They are not intended to instruct the farmer in methods of working or to help him arrange his programme of activity as were the much more detailed lists given by Columella and Palladius. They simply state what is done on the farm at a specific time of the year. It has been suggested,[6] however, that such passages as Cato II, 1, where he writes of inspecting the farm to see in what condition it is, 'operaque quae facta infectaque sient' imply the existence of a written work-schedule known both to the owner and his *vilicus*. The word 'infecta' is significant of a prior assignment with which the present achievement is being compared. In II, 6, Cato is more explicit about this: 'quae opera fieri velit et quae locari velit, uti imperet et ea scripta relinquat'. Varro (I, 36) advises that such a list of tasks should be displayed on the farm.

Although the *Menologia* were found in Rome, they could nevertheless relate to a cooler region without necessarily coming from very far away. They could, for example, belong to the Faliscan countryside or to farms in the foothills of the Apennines to the north-east of Rome. This would allow for a significant difference in climate on high ground. The mention of sheep-rearing in these inscriptions is concentrated upon the months of April and May, and 'oves lustrantur' appears as an important event, parallel to the 'vindemiae' in October. If these calendars were designed for individual farms or regions these belong to a sheep-rearing community. If they came from either of the districts mentioned above, the flocks would have been moved to the higher pastures in May, and this might account for the sparsity of references to sheep-shearing.

The Calendar which has been found beneath S. Maria Maggiore in Rome is incomplete, but originally consisted of a list of the dates for each month together with festivals, and indications of the work to be done on the farm. This was accompanied by wall-paintings depicting the activities appropriate to the various months. The portions of this calendar which remain belong mainly to the latter half of the year, one of the clearest sections being the month of September. Activities depicted for this month include fruit-picking, for which an interesting curved ladder is being used.

The Calendar has been dated to the first half of the fourth century AD, on the basis of the detail in the illustrations and of the mention of the *Ludi Sarmatici* among the festivals.[7] Magi (*Il Calendario*, p. 59ff) considers that the building in which this calendar was found was originally a *macellum* and suggests its identification as the *Macellum Liviae,* thus placing the original construction in the first century AD. There are difficulties in this theory, which have been discussed by H. Mielsch (*Gnomon,* Vol. 48, 1976, 499-504), who thinks it possible that the original building was a bathing establishment or a private house. A calendar of this nature would be appropriately placed in a *macellum* to which the *rustici* came to sell their produce, though other evidence suggests that it would have been more likely to find a place on a private estate or even in a dwelling. The advice of Varro, *Res Rusticae* I, 36, 'quae dixi scripta et proposita habere in villa oportet maxime ut vilicus norit' has been thought to imply that such lists of farm activities and illustrations of them (proposita) were common as an aid to efficiency on large farms. It is probable, however, that 'scripta et proposita' simply means 'written and displayed'. The same impression regarding the display of farming instructions may be obtained from Petronius, *Satyricon* 30, 3-4. This describes a calendar which was on the wall of Trimalchio's dining-room. There were two posts, each of which had two tablets fixed to it, and one of these tablets was inscribed:

'III et prid. Kal. Ian. C. noster foras cenat.'
The other had the phases of the moon on it and seven pictures of stars, 'et qui dies boni quique incommodi essent, distinguente bulla notabantur'. (30, 4)). This certainly resembles the *Menologia,* though the use of the 'bulla' is reminiscent of the *parapegmata* (Degrassi, *Inscr. Italiae,* XIII, 2). The mention of the two posts may be significant: if so, it implies that such calendars were usually displayed out-of-doors rather than in dining-rooms.

Varro does not divide the farmer's year into months, but into eight periods of work, starting from February 7th which he regards as the first day of Spring. J. E. Skydsgaard[8] thinks that Varro did not follow the civil year in his arrangement because, prior to the reform of the calendar by Julius Caesar, it was unsatisfactory for farmers (p. 19). 'Our treatise is written *after* Caesar's reform, but the *dramatic* date is considerably earlier — in other words *before* the reform.' In any case it seems probable that farmers would not immediately change their customs in this matter until the new calendar was well-known and established throughout the countryside. There is much variation in the way in which ancient authors treat this subject. Pliny (*N.H.* XVIII, 220-320) uses the same arrangement but begins on November 10th. Columella's calendar (XI, 2, 3-101) is divided into half-months, for greater accuracy, but also perhaps to take account of the waxing and waning of the moon. The month was originally so divided by the Greeks.[9] This calendar is intended to show the work of the *vilicus* on an estate, and therefore does not include a detailed account of the cultivation of the *hortus* or kitchen-garden.

In the *Georgics* of Virgil, as in Hesiod's *Works and Days* the didactic intention is apparent, as is also the close connection with the life of the working farmer. For the countryman, cultivating his own plot and living close to the soil, much of this information was not explicitly taught, rather passed on from father to son or from master to slave. For example, the weather signs in *Georgics* I do not begin, even in the poem, as ways of determining the conditions likely to be encountered tomorrow, but as indications of the time for carrying out particular tasks on the farm. When the snow beings to melt on the mountains and the warmer winds make the ground friable (*Georgics* I, 43 and 45) one should begin ploughing.

'Libra die somnique pares ubi fecerit horas
et medium luci atque umbris iam dividet orbem' (208-9)
barley should be sown. The point being made is that the farmer knows when to undertake these tasks. It is questionable whether the Italian farmer made as much use of astronomical data as Virgil does. Pliny refers to him as 'indocilis caeli' (*N.H.* XVIII, 60 (226)). The literary influence of Aratus, the habits of the sea-going Greeks and contemporary scientific interests probably account for the emphasis given to the observation of the constellations. The progress of the seasons, however, helps the farmer to

decide upon the timing of his main activities and to this extent the constellations — and the calendar — are relevant. Virgil in true poetic fashion, is making explicit what was normally an intuitive or at any rate an unformulated response made by the farmer to certain environmental conditions. D. F. Thomson in '*The Seasonal Factor in Human Culture*'[10] discusses with reference to an Australian tribe the seasonal activities undertaken by primitive peoples. This was a food-gathering tribe, not practising agriculture, but Thomson shows that they knew by tradition and personal experience when each of their many foodstuffs would be available. In the same way Virgil's farmer would know

'quo sidere terram
vertere . . . ulmisque adiungere vitis
conveniat'. (1-3).

Columella may have been thinking of the Georgics and similar accounts in which astronomy was emphasised when he stated in Book XI, 2, 2, that the farmer was not to observe the time of year in the same way as the astronomer. He need not wait for the fixed day which is supposed to mark the beginning of Spring. He can take advantage of the warmer weather as soon as it comes, even in January: he can do some cultivating on January 13th. This is where Columella begins his calendar, and it ends suitably with December and early January. In December the soil is not to be disturbed with any iron tool, nor is it to be touched in the early days of January, except that a symbolic start may be made to the year's work on January 1st for good luck.

In Palladius much of the advice on general cultivation resembles that of Columella, but he includes in his book, which is itself a calendar, more information about gardening and the preservation of food. He expounds the scope of the work in I, 1, 2: it concerns 'omni genere eorum quae vel facere vel nutrire oportet agricolam ratione voluptatis et fructus . . .' Information 'de hortis' appears in a separate section of each chapter, and the variety of vegetables discussed, as well as the detail of the accounts, is noteworthy. In February, the time for sowing most hardy vegetables, we find: 'de lactuca, carduo, nasturtio, coriandro, papavero, allio, ulpico, de satureia cum disciplina, item de cepullis, similiter de anetho, senapi, de caulibus cum disciplina sua et de asparagis, de malva, menta, feniculo, pastinaca, cunela, cerefolio, beta, porro cum disciplina, de inula et colocaseis similiter'.[11] Further items, to be sown in March, are armoracea, origanum, beta, cappari, intuba, rafanus, melones, cucumis, ruta, cucurbita, blitum, anesum and cyminus.[12] Such spaces as are left in the garden by May are there for a purpose, VI, 5, 'Hortorum spatia, quae per autumnum seminibus inplenda destinantur aut plantis, nunc conveniet pastinare.' By June further sowings will require irrigation. The gardener is to collect his own seed from the varieties he favours, 'ex his ergo semina colligemus' (IX, 2). Caution is advised: 'in novo enim genere seminum ante experimentum non est spes tota ponenda' (I, 6).

The instructions in Book I indicate the readership for which the book was intended. The preface (I, 1) is short because it is not a good idea to talk in rhetorical fashion to 'rusticis', but the 'second preface', in I, 6, somewhat contradicts this. A number of precepts are offered here which are clearly intended for owners or their *vilici*. In I, 6, 2, 'rusticos 'is used of employees, as distinct from those in charge to whom the passage is addressed. Yet even here details useful mainly to the field worker are included, such as 'in omni opere inserendi, putandi ac recidendi, duris et acutis utere ferramentis' (I, 6, 4), and 'omnis incisura sarmenti avertatur a gemma ne eam stilla, quae fluere consuevit, extinguat' (I, 6, 9). On the other hand in the same section we find advice to the owner or tenant: 'domino vel colono confinia possidenti, qui fundum vel agrum suum locat, damnis suis ac litibus studet. in agro periclitantur interiora, nisi colantur extrema' (I, 6, 6). The use of *dominus* and *colonus* as alternatives in this passage is interesting. Both could occupy land, and both were concerned with safeguarding their boundaries against encroachment. Palladius is also addressing the prospective owner in I, 7, on choosing land, and in I, 8, on building. The conclusion must be that Palladius' work, though able to interest the absentee landowner, is mainly addressed to the owner or tenant who is involved in the practical details of farming. The information could, of course, be transmitted by him to his employees, but to do this successfully he must himself have possessed some knowledge and experience of the work. The amount of experimentation recommended, however, and the variety of the produce suggests that some at least of the advice was originally addressed to proprietors of large estates or would even have been of use to those growing for the market. The stress upon the quality of the fruit and vegetables grown also implies this, as do such specialities as 'uvae sine seminibus' (III, 29).

How much of the information given by the agronomists is relevant to the activities of the smallholder? Columella is anxious to show that farming is a pursuit fit for gentlemen (Preface 1, 10), but he is also aware of what could be done by those in less fortunate circumstances. He mentions for instance that Regulus had once been 'Pupiniae pestilentis simul et exilis agri cultorem' (I, 4, 3). Abandoned plots can be restored, 'seu sponte seu quolibet casu derelicta humus, cum est repetita cultu, magno faenore cessatorum colono respondet (II, 1, 3) — though even here his metaphor 'magno faenore' betrays his familiarity with commercial enterprise. He knows that land newly brought under cultivation is very fruitful at first, but 'mox deinde non ita respondere labori colonorum' (II, 1, 5). He is discussing the affairs of *coloni* now, not of the *dominus*. The *rustici*, he says (II, 9, 10) soak their seed-corn before sowing it in the juice of the *sedum* (house leek) to ward off pests. They can sow *cantherinum* (a variety of barley) which provides a good feed for animals, and is better for humans than bad wheat, 'nec aliud in egenis rebus magis inopiam defendit'. He discusses panic and millet 'nam multis regionibus cibariis eorum coloni sustinentur' (II, 9, 17) 'Regionibus' here is often taken to mean 'foreign countries', but there seems no reason why it cannot refer to parts of Italy.[13] Pliny (XVIII, 10 (53-55)) writes at some length about these grains and states (54) 'panis multifariam et a milio fit, e panico rarus'. The choice between provender for animals and food for men is hardly one which would have to be made by the gentleman farmer, but in II, 11, 7 Columella refers to this, 'Neque est rustici prudentis magis pabulis studere pecudum quam cibis hominum, cum praesertim liceat illa quoque cultu pratorum consequi'. The first part of this sentence sounds like a quotation from traditional country lore, and it is followed, as so often, by an additional comment which is Columella's own. Surely the small farmer is envisaged in the advice about substitutes for manure (II, 14, 6) which includes collecting and heaping up leaves, gathering them from bramble thickets and 'viis compitisque'. He can cut down bracken without harming his neighbour, perhaps even doing him a good turn. This can be mixed with farmyard sweepings and stored in a trench. The antiquity of this method is indicated by the addition of a magical 'serpent scarer' to the heap — a suggestion for which our literary evidence goes back to Varro (I, 38, 3): 'In eo, si in medio robusta aliqua materia sit depacta negant serpentem nasci'. This could originally have been a method of letting air into the compost heap. This passage is concerned with hill-farming: 'Nec ignoro quoddam esse ruris genus, in quo neque pecora neque aves haberi possint'.

The most numerous references in our literary sources to work on the smallholding are to be found in discussion of the *hortus*, which was largely, though not entirely, devoted to the growing of vegetables. It is within this section that Columella's calendar is placed, though detailed study of the cultivation of herbs and other food plants is to be found in Book XII. Wild as well as cultivated varieties are included, and methods of preserving them appear both in Columella and in the parallel books of Pliny's *Natural History* (chiefly XVIII and XIX). The Marsian onion, which the *rustici* call 'unio', the service-apples to be picked by hand and sealed up in little jars, then buried in a trench; apples and figs as an important part of the winter food supply; the fodder plant which the *rustici* call *faenum Graecum* — all these are derived from the traditions of the small farm. The garden can be enclosed by a hedge of thorn bushes, 'ratio maxime antiquis probata' (Col. X1, 3, 3-7). It is possible to obtain much information about the work of the smallholder from the agronomists, whose incidental remarks upon it are included for various reasons. They are there:

    i. for their antiquarian interest;
    ii. because they have been adopted as common practice;

iii. to contribute to the complete picture of Italian agriculture which a conscientious writer wishes to produce.

The third reason is particularly applicable to an author such as the Elder Pliny, whose desire to amass and publish knowledge for its own sake is paramount. Whatever their motives, however, they have conveyed to us a surprising amount of information regarding a section of the population which was seldom influential and was unlikely to have any direct acquaintance with their works.

Notes to Chapter Three

1. M. Rostovtzeff, *Social and Economic History of the Roman Empire*, 1957, Vol. I, plate XXXVI.
2. CIL VI, 2305 and 2306.
3. Degrassi. *Inscri. Italiae*, Vol. XIII, 2, p. 284.
4. Wissowa, *Römische Bauernkalender*, Apophoreton, XLVII, Berlin, 1903, p. 45. A. L. Broughton, *The Menologia Rustica*, *Classical Philology* XXXI, 1936, suggested that the calendars might belong to the plains around the River Po in N. Italy. This raises problems, such as the inclusion of olive-growing, which is not possible where the average temperature in the coldest months falls below 3°C.
5. As regards the importance of waterproofing jars it should be noted that there are no less than six chapters on the subject in the *Geoponika* (VI, 4-9).
6. K. D. White, *Roman Agricultural Writers I*, *Varro and his Predecessors* in *Aufstieg und Niedergang der Römischen Welt*, IV, 1973, p. 454-5, mentions the idea of a work-schedule in another context.
7. F. Magi, *Memorie della Pontificia Accademia romana di Archeologia*, series III, Vol. XI, 1972, pp. 27 and 39.
8. *Varro the Scholar*, *Analecta Romana Instituti Danici*, IV, Suppl., 1968, p. 19.
9. T. A. Sinclair, *Hesiod, Works and Days*, p. 80, note to line 768.
10. *Proceedings of the Prehistoric Society*, V, 1939, p. 209-221.
11 The plants are: lettuce, cardoon, cress, coriander, poppy, garlic, ulpicum (a form of leek), savory, onion, dill, mustard, cabbage, asparagus, mallow, mint, fennel, parsnip, cunila, chervil, beet, leek, elecampane.
12. These are: horseradish, marjoram, beet, caper, endive, radish, melon, cucumber, rue, gourd, blitum (a leaf vegetable), dill, cumin.
13. cf. VIII, 8, 1, 'longinquis regionibus', with reference to the keeping of pigeons.

CHAPTER FOUR

Wild and Cultivated Plants: a note on the peasant economy of Roman Italy

It has long been surmised that the Italian peasant in the Roman period could not have subsisted entirely upon his *heredium*, even when it was considerably more than two *iugera*. Juvenal was speaking for many of those before him, as well as for his own contemporaries when he said of the traditional allocation:

'Nunc modus hic agri nostro non sufficit horto'.

(*Satires* XIV, 172.)

Yet amid much speculation upon this point one aspect of the countryman's livelihood seems to have attracted little attention. In addition to any other resources he had the use of the wild plants of the extensive forests, the mountains, pastures and fallow fields. In general, food obtained from wild plants did not in Roman times, any more than it does in Italy today, take the

This chapter was published as an article in JRS, LXV, 1975.

place of grain, the staple article of diet. This may account for Pliny's statement in the *Natural History* XXI, 50 (86) where, after mentioning the large number of 'herbae sponte nascentes' used for food by other peoples, he writes: 'In Italia paucissimas novimus, fraga, tamnum (wild vine), ruscum (butcher's broom), batim marinam (samphire), batim hortensiam, quam aliqui asparagum Gallicum vocant . . .' Such a remark seems astonishing in view of the numerous other examples Pliny himself has previously given,[1] but its interpretation depends on the meaning to be assigned to the word *cibus,* as well as on the limiting effect of the phrase 'herbae sponte nascentes', which may not include all the plants we call 'wild'. It is clear from the conclusion of the paragraph cited above, where 'oblectamenta' are compared with 'cibos', that *cibi* is being used here to mean 'staple food'.[2]

Wild plants supplied the deficiencies of a farinaceous diet, and added a relish to the plain fare. This is made clear in relation to primitive peoples, both ancient and modern, by G. W. Dimbleby,[3] who remarks that the wild flora contains many more plants which can be used for flavouring than are cultivated in herb gardens. However before we can discuss the use of wild plants for food in Roman times, we must consider whether the Romans distinguished between wild and cultivated plants in the same way as we do.

The word 'wild' in reference to plants is usually *silvestris,* while 'cultivated' is *sativus. Silvestris* appears in its primary meaning to refer not to the way in which the plant is treated, as does *sativus,* but to the place in which it grows. It is not easy to find a parallel for this expression in Greek. The Greek word for 'wild', whether describing plants or animals, is ἄγριος and its opposite is ἥμερος. Derivatives from ὕλη seem not to bear the connotation of 'wild', but rather to retain their connection with 'wood' in some form. ὑλαῖος may be an exception to this, but it was not in common use in prose in any of its meanings. It is unlikely that all the plants described as *silvestris* ever grew in woodlands. Rather we may assume that in the formative period of the Latin language the uninhabited areas were mostly forested — therefore a plant which grew outside the cultivated lands was *silvestris.*[4] It is true that there are certain special uses of the noun *silva*, as for example where it describes a quantity or 'forest' of weapons or other items, but this is clearly derived from its literal meaning of 'woodland'. It can also denote a wild area on an estate, a contrived 'wilderness' as in Columella, *De Re Rustica* XI, 2, 83: 'Tum etiam silvam si quis barbaricam, id est consemineam velit facere, recte conseret glandibus et ceteris seminibus'. Again the connection with 'forest' is clear. Varro gives a precise definition of *silvestris*: 'Itaque ita esse docent silvestria, ad quae sator non accessit.'[5] The use of 'accessit' here is interesting — the cultivator has not reached them. What will he do when he finds them: collect the seeds, foster the plants where they are, or transplant them to his own plot?

Some plants which we should call 'wild', because they are 'herbae sponte nascentes', are not described by the adjective *silvestris*. Pliny says of the poppy:[6] 'Inter sativa et silvestria medium genus, quoniam in arvis sed sponte nasceretur, rhoeam vocavimus et erraticum'. Wild plants growing on arable land, whether or not *sponte*, are often called *agrestis*, which corresponds to ἀρουραῖος in Theophrastus.[7] Not only the poppy comes into this 'medium genus', as we see from Cato (*De Agri Cultura* 149, 2). He is laying down terms of lease for winter pasturage. These include:

'Bubus domitis binis, cantherio uni cum emptor pascet, domino pascere recipitur; holeris, asparagis, lignis, aqua, itinere, actu domini usioni recipitur.'

The whole paragraph concerns pasture-land (pratum), so the *holus* and *asparagi* cannot be garden produce. Their proximity in the sentence to 'lignis, aqua, itinere, actu' also suggests a natural resource rather than a cultivated product. The passage in fact implies that it was usual to collect wild or semi-wild greens for food, and the owner was permitted to do this even if he had let the grazing to someone else. Or, as the cook in Plautus' *Pseudolus* expresses it: 'Quas herbas pecudes non edunt, homines edunt.'[8] Seneca, *De Providentia* III, 6, seems to be picturing Fabricius as engaged in this task of gathering wild food-plants on arable land:

'Infelix est Fabricius, quod rus suum, quantum a re publica vacavit, fodit? quod bellum tam cum Pyrrho quam cum divitiis gerit? quod ad focum cenat illas ipsas radices et herbas quas in repurgando agro triumphalis senex vulsit?'

This could describe a process of gleaning rather than picking wild plants, but if so the field contained a very mixed crop — 'radices et herbas'.

Columella is interesting on the subject of wild or semi-wild plants. In XII, 7, 1, writing of methods of pickling herbs, he includes alexanders (*olusatrum*), capers, 'pastinacae agrestis vel sativae cum coliculo silentem florem' (parsnip), asparagus, butcher's broom, bryony, in fact a long list of plants, any or all of which might have been 'wild' in our sense of the word, while others would grow on pasture-land, privately or publicly owned. Of the caper Columella says: 'cultu aut nullo aut levissimo contenta est, quippe quae res etiam in desertis agris citra rustici operam convalescat.'[9] He also tells us how to prevent it spreading if it is planted in the kitchen garden. The buds from wild caper plants are still collected and pickled or used in sauces at the present day. In XII, 8, 3, Columella writes of pepperwort: 'sunt qui sativi vel etiam silvestris lepidii herbam cum collegerunt in umbra siccent, deinde folia eius, abiecto caule, die et nocte muria macerata expressaque lacti misceant sine condimentis . . .' In the next sentence the *satureia* (savory) is described as *comperta* — found, discovered, therefore presumably growing wild. Wild plums and cornel berries are among the many other items preserved.

We have already cited passages from Cato and Columella which mention asparagus. With them should be included the remark of Cato: 'Ibi corrudam serito unde asparagi fiant.'[10] *Corruda* is the name given to the wild form of asparagus,[11] from which Cato here seems to be suggesting that the cultivated form may be produced. He may simply regard 'asparagus' as the name of the edible portion, and be saying no more than Martial (*Epig*. XIII, 21):

> 'Mollis in aequorea quae crevit spina Ravenna
> non erit incultis gratior asparagis.'

Pliny seems to regard Cato's remark as explaining the origin of the cultivated plant: 'De origine eorum e silvestribus corrudis abunde dictum et quomodo eos iuberet Cato in harundinetis

seri'.[12] However, Columella refers to the wild form as 'quam
corrudam rustici vocant'. (XI, 3, 43). Palladius gives some advice
about the growing of wild asparagus:

'Mihi etiam illud utile videtur ac diligens, ut asparagi agrestis
radices plurimas in unum locum congeramus cultum vel certe
saxosum, quae statim fructum dent ex loco, qui aliud nihil
alebat, et has annis omnibus incendamus in scopis, ut fructus
frequentior surgat et fortior. hoc autem genus est sapore
iucundius.' (III, 24, 8.)

Palladius is not referring to a primitive custom, but making a
practical suggestion for his contemporaries who wanted to enjoy
wild asparagus as a delicacy. Yet the method he describes arises
naturally from earlier practice and tradition.[18]

Virgil, writing in *Georgics* II, 47ff, of the cultivation of trees,
describes how the wild varieties ('sponte sua quae se tollunt in
luminis oras') can be improved either by grafting or by removing
them to prepared ground:

'tamen haec quoque, si quis
inserat aut scrobibus mandet mutata subactis,
exuerint silvrestrem animum, cultugue frequenti
in quascumque voles artis haud tarda sequentur.'

In the next two lines he added that the rootstock which has not
as yet produced any fruit will do so when, removed from the
woodland, it has room to grow:

'nec non et sterilis quae stirpibus exit ab imis,
hoc faciat, vacuos si sit digesta per agros.'

Columella describes explicitly a process of domestication, this
time with reference to a herb. For he says that if the mint you
have sown fails to grow 'licet de novalibus silvestre mentastrum
conligere, atque ita inversis cacuminibus disponere; quae res
feritatem detrahit, atque edomitam reddit'.[14] 'Inversis cacuminibus' may be simply a magical touch,[15] or it may be a way of
disposing of the wild foliage and retarding further growth until
the roots have benefited from their new environment. There may
be a trace of this idea in Theophrastus, I, 6, 10, with reference to
the arum.[16] In this passage he states that some people turn arum
plants upside down before the leaves have started to grow, and

that this is done to make the roots stronger and to encourage their growth.

The clearest statements about cultivation of wild plants are to be found in Palladius. The first example we shall consider is in XI, 4: 'item betam locis siccioribus nec non armoraceam (wild radish) seremus vel transferemus ad culta, ut melior fiat: nam haec agrestis est rafanus'. Here it seems likely that 'transferemus ad culta' means 'we shall transplant (from the wild) to cultivated plots (or cultivation)'. It could simply refer to transplanting seedlings within the confines of a garden, as it often does. But the use of the word *transferre*, as we shall see, is characteristic of passages in which plants are being moved from wild places to cultivation, and the use of *agrestis* in the last part of the sentence supports this connection in the above passage. An example of this is found in Palladius XI, 3. 'si transferendis plantis nodum facias in radice, sessiles fient'. This picturesque idea would be impossible to carry out with either cuttings or small seedlings, as the roots would not be long or sturdy enough to tie in a knot. That these words record a practice of great antiquity is also probable because they include what is really a reference to sympathetic magic. The farmer hopes that the plant will take hold upon the soil as firmly as the knot is tied.

In III, 25, 29, after an account of growing the *morus* (mulberry) from seed, Palladius says: 'plantam, si robustam, transferes mense octobri et novembri, si teneram, februario et martio. scrobes desiderat altiores, intervalla maiora, ne umbris prematur alterius'. This surely suggests transferring a plant which is already growing, either wild or in another garden or part of the same garden.[17] There seems to be no indication in any of these passages that an old plant is being divided. *Planta*, though it usually means a cutting or a sucker, must here mean a well-grown plant, especially when it is described as 'robustam'. The same use of *planta* is found in X, 13, 'hoc mense ultimo thymum seremus, sed melius plantis nascitur, quamvis possit et semine'. Thyme does not lend itself to the taking of cuttings, as its stems are short and brittle. It spreads quickly and forms large cushions, so that a portion of a well-grown plant, wild or cultivated, can be broken off and transplanted. Such pieces would very easily be obtained from the garigue in many parts of Italy, as Pliny suggests that they were in Greece.[18] Cultivated and wild thyme are mentioned by Columella, who says that they 'studiose conseruntur' only by bee-keepers. Thyme can be grown in gardens, he tells us, and it is better to use young plants than to sow it. 'Locum neque pinguem neque stercoratum, sed apricum desiderant, ut quae macerrimo solo per se maritimis regionibus nascantur.'[19] When the plants have been set in the ground they should be watered with water in which a crushed stalk of thyme has been soaked: sympathetic magic again. It may well be that magic is chiefly found in these agricultural treatises in connection with the older and more basic operations, because it was in association with these in the distant past that magical practices arose.

Another example of *transferre* in the sense of moving a wild plant to cultivation is found in Pliny XIX, 5 (23). Here he is describing a method of growing cucumbers, which as he says is also given by Columella (XI, 3, 53). For our present purpose it is the planting of the bramble, not the cucumber, that is important:

'Fruticem rubi quam vastissimum in apricum locum transferre et recidere duum digitorum relicta stirpe circa vernum aequi-noctium; ita in medulla rubi semine cucumeris insito terra minuta fimoque circumaggeratas resistere frigori radices.'

In Columella's more professional account, fennels and brambles are to be planted in alternate rows and used in this way. The word *transferre* is not used by Columella, though he probably does mean wild fennels and brambles. His account seems to be more suitable for the requirements of large-scale producers. Pliny gives the instructions in reference to a single plant, and in his account the method appears more appropriate for use on a small scale, in the way in which no doubt it began. For a garden in which the wild species mix happily with cultivated plants, however, we need look no further than Columella's poem in Book X, where *eruca* (colewort), sorrel, squill and wild asparagus are mingled with leeks, parsley, cucumbers and other cultivated varieties. Yet the wild plants are not there because of neglect, for this garden is described in line 424 as 'excultus'.

There seem to have been three types of wild plant, not always considered separately by Roman writers, but which can be differentiated: those which grow outside the bounds of cultivation or fallow land or pasture; those found on pasture-land; those growing in fallow fields. Plants in the last two categories may not all be growing *sponte,* that is, without human aid or intervention. It is worth recalling here the very varied and sturdy collection of plants to be found growing in pockets of unused arable land throughout the Mediterranean area in the Spring. It is also useful to remember that in antiquity, as in the remoter areas even today, such plants did not have to contend with the powerful modern weed-killers. These diminutive meadows are described by Columella when he is suggesting suitable conditions for the keeping of bees. 'Mille praeterea semina vel crudo cespite virentia, vel subacta sulco, flores amicissimos apibus creant . . .'[20] Again: 'Iam vero notae vilioris innumerabiles nascuntur herbae cultis atque pascuis regionibus, quae favorum ceras exuberant.' Columella is only concerned here with plants attractive to bees, but even so he lists a considerable number.[21]

Pliny in the last chapter of Book XX says he is about to leave 'garden-plants' (*hortensiis*). But he has written of almost as many wild as cultivated varieties in that book. Often in respect of herbal remedies he considers the wild variety better than the cultivated. This may be true in some cases, but it may also reflect the fact that these recipes were originally devised for wild plants. In *The Geography of Domestication* Erich Isaac suggests that some plants used by the ancients may not have been domesticated at all, because obtaining the plant was part of the curative process. A cultivated plant would not have the same potency as a rare specimen growing in a wild and remote place.[22] Even in the last years of the Roman Empire the collecting of wild plants by individuals for immediate use as remedies seems to have continued. Marcellus Empiricus, who lived in the reigns of Theodosius I and II, says that he has not only obtained remedies from authors such as Pliny and Celsus 'sed etiam ab agrestibus et plebeis remedia fortuita atque simplicia, quae experimentis probaverunt, didici.' (*Praef.,* 2).[23] The large variety of herbs mentioned is notable, even

if only those locally available in Italy are counted. It is clear that
the physician or even the patient is expected to be able to find
them. For instance, in XXIII, 71, instructions are given for recog-
nising and picking the caper root.

Some of the above examples seem to suggest that there are in
the work of Pliny and other Roman writers on agriculture and
horticulture traces of very early food-gathering and gardening
practices. They are not for the most part attributed by these
writers to past generations, but offered to their contemporaries
as possible alternative methods, or sometimes as the universal way
of cultivating a particular plant. It seems therefore that they were
either still in use at the time, or if derived from another literary
source, they were in use when that was written. The period in
which wild and cultivated plants were not fully differentiated in
Europe, and when an intermediate category existed, has usually
been regarded as earlier than the classical age of Rome. J. G. D.
Clarke refers to it, '. . . under primitive conditions the distinction
between 'wild' and 'domesticated' plants is often slight and a
multitude of gradations in status may exist between wild, protected and fully domesticated species.'[24] In his *Histoire de L'Alimentation végétale* Adam Maurizio includes a list[25] of 'Plantes du
Ramassage' in which there are 621 separate items, each accompanied by details concerning the sources of information. These
consist of wild plants used for food in prehistoric times, those
still used by primitive peoples, and those used in time of food
shortage in Europe in the years 1914-18. The Roman period is
not specifically treated in this work, though many of the plants
tabulated are mentioned by Roman authors as being used in this
way. One of the reasons why the Romans are omitted from such
lists is given by Jacques André, *L'Alimentation et La Cuisine à
Rome* (p. 22) with reference to the plants he himself is enumer-
ating. He thinks that the Romans must have used many more
wild roots and bulbs for food than appear in his own lists, but they
are not mentioned in the surviving literature because the authors
belonged to the upper classes of society. They were therefore
unfamiliar with the technique of obtaining food from the wild.
This does not seem to apply to Galen, who discusses wild food-

plants as freely as he does the cultivated varieties. In this way *De Alimentorum Facultatibus* and *De Probis Pravisque Alimentorum Succis* differ from any modern book on dietetics. In the former he writes for example of plants of the thistle type:

'Ἀνίσχοντα τῆς γῆς ἄρτι τὰ τοιαῦτα φυτά, πρὶν εἰς ἀκάνθας αὐτῶν τελευτῆσαι τὰ φύλλα, πολλοὶ τῶν ἀγροίκων ἐσθίουσιν (L. p. 635). οὐκ ὠμὰ μόνον, ἀλλὰ καὶ δι' ὕδατος ἕψοντες.'

In *De Probis Pravisque Alimentorum Succis* he discusses pine kernels as food. Although Galen considers, as for example in *De Alimentorum Facultatibus* II, 38, p. 621 (Teubner), that most wild plants provide very little nourishment, he again and again finds it necessary to discuss them, and he distinguishes between those which are used διὰ λιμὸν and those which are used χωρὶς λιμοῦ (II, 64).

II

For purposes of comparison we may consider the situation not long after the Roman period as described by Georges Duby.[26] He draws attention to the scattered settlement of seventh-century Europe, when only a small amount of land was under continuous cultivation. He considers that at this time the peasants derived only a part of their livelihood from agriculture, the rest being obtained by fishing, hunting and gathering wild fruits in the surrounding waste lands and forests. Duby sees this situation as the result of technological weaknesses which prevented agriculture from becoming sufficiently productive in the period with which he is dealing. It seems likely that this was a problem of long standing.

Within the Roman period it is not only probable that wild plants were extensively used for food in Italy but it is also possible that there was an intermediate stage in which a plant was protected and used though not actually transplanted from the wild. This is sometimes the case nowadays with bushes of rosemary, and the writer of the Virgilian poem *Culex* may be referring to the practice of caring for wild rosemary near the cottage when he says: 'et roris non avia cura marini'. The idea mentioned by Pliny of sowing what he calls *hipposelinum* (alexanders) in

uncultivated land near a stone wall is probably another instance
of the protection of a wild plant. Often however wild plants used
for food would become established near dwellings in the areas
where the refuse from meals was deposited. Erich Isaac (op. cit.,
p. 27) thinks that, in the primitive setting, if property rights
were so strong that they were protected even in the absence of the
owners, a similar idea of possession may have attached to certain
plants which were considered to belong to individuals or small
groups. Such a custom could have formed part of the process
of development to which André refers (op. cit., p. 50).

In *Plants and Archaeology*, p. 39, G. W. Dimbleby writes that
it is difficult to produce 'incontrovertible proof' of the association
between wild species and man. This is said with reference to more
primitive societies, but many of the plants discussed (especially
on p. 32) are also mentioned by Roman writers as being useful
for food in their wild or transplanted form. Dimbleby also suggests that it would be simple to transfer a useful plant from a
remote spot to a place nearer one's home, and that this is being
done today in tropical gardens. It seems that it was also being
done in Roman Italy at a time when true cultivation was already
established. The instructions given by the agronomists about the
growing of grain and the cultivation of the vine suggest a much
more developed technique. These were also the province of the
commercial grower. The work of the Roman agricultural writers
may therefore be said to contain material representing two very
different levels of culture.

Wild vegetables tend to be tougher and more fibrous than
cultivated varieties,[27] and in the early stages of cultivation much
of the toughness would be retained. Galen, whose low opinion of
vegetables seems until recently to have exercised a strong influence
upon European diet, warns his readers against wild and cultivated
varieties alike. Their roots περιττωματικαί τε εἰσι καὶ δύσπεπτοι[28].
He is also worried about the wild varieties being dry.[29] Some can
be improved by steeping and boiling, as he says of the asphodel:
ἐγὼ δ'οἶδα διὰ λιμὸν ἀγροίκους τινὰς ἐψήσεσί τε πλείοσι καὶ ἀποβρέξεσιν
ἐν ὕδατι γλυκεῖ μόλις αὐτὴν ἐδώδιμον ἐργασαμένους.[30]
However the buds of any plant may be eaten: καλλίους δ'αὐτῶν εἰσιν

οἱ τῆς τερμίνθου τε καὶ ἄγνου καὶ ἀμπέλου καὶ σχοίνου καὶ βάτου καὶ κυνοσβάτου.

(*De Alimentorum Facultatibus* II, 60). The toughness may also account for the vigorous pounding recommended in ancient recipes, and described in the *Moretum*[31] lines 111-112. Earlier in the poem (94ff) the poet recounts in great detail the process of removing the outer skins of the garlic, as if this was in itself a particularly important and interesting activity. In Ovid's account of a *moretum* being offered to Cybele (*Fasti* IV, 304):

'candidus elisae miscetur caseus herbae'

the use of *elisae* indicates the crushing of the vegetables, and the next line:

'cognoscat priscos ut dea cibos'

emphasises the antiquity of such a process. The descriptions of the various kinds of lettuce by the agronomists are also noteworthy in relation to the question of texture and toughness. Pliny says that the wild varieties of lettuce all have rough stalks and leaves.[32] He lists at least five wild varieties which can be used for medicinal purposes. Two are said to grow 'in arvis'. With reference to one of his remedies Pliny says: 'quidam et e sativis colligunt sucum minus efficacem.'[33] There are also instructions in Pliny, XIX, 38 (131) for blanching lettuce, which may have been necessary when tough or strongly-flavoured varieties were commonly used. Nowadays it is more usual to blanch endive than lettuce, because it is more bitter.

Pliny would probably have explained the frequent use of the pestle and mortar in Roman cookery in a different way. In XIX, 19 (58) he suggests that salads (not *moretum* here but *acetaria*, pickled salad vegetables) were eaten in earlier times because they needed no cooking and saved fuel. However the emphasis upon the steeping and pounding of vegetables is very noticeable in Roman writings on horticulture and cookery. It could well have become traditional owing to the use originally of wild varieties, even if they were produced in cultivated plots.

The practices which have been discussed here form only a very small part of the traditional lore used by the Italian peasant to enable his to subsist on a poor or scanty land-holding. They suggest that the stage of transition from food-gathering to cultivation in Italy may have continued into Roman times. Yet at any particular date within this period regional differences must have been very marked. Even if we discount those crops and techniques which clearly belong to the realm of the market-gardener in the suburban areas of Latium and Campania, we must take note of the various climatic zones of Italy and the remoteness of the *montani*. To take just one example, Liguria, we have a description of land use there in *Communità rurali nell'Italia antica* by Emilio Sereni (Rome, 1955), p. 539. Sereni writes of the different types of land to be found in Liguria in antiquity, and of particular interest to us here is his mention of the *debbi* — plots of land once cultivated but now in process of dereliction or actually abandoned. He emphasises how quickly one can pass to a different type of land, where there are no specific boundaries between forest, woodland pastures, *macchia* and moorland.

III

Our ancient literary sources contain statements of two distinct types concerning wild food-plants. First, there is advice to the comparatively affluent Roman reader on the ways in which wild herbs and vegetables can be used to enhance the attractions of an already well-supplied table. Secondly there are accounts of peasant usage, either contemporary or archaic, in which both wild and cultivated plants form a necessary part of a subsistence economy. There is also mention of the enforced use of a wider variety of plants in time of scarcity.[34] The use of terms implying 'wild' and 'cultivated' by Latin authors does not correspond exactly with our own categories and reflects the more varied sources of the food-supply in ancient times. It may indeed be arguable that such terms as *silvestris* and *sativus* first attained precise definition in medical and magical works, that is in contexts where the distinction was felt to be particularly important. We have found the customs of the poor chiefly among those attributed to the *rustici*, the *pastores* and the *veteres*. The *veteres* may have lived a few generations before the writer who quotes them, but that will still bring them within the Roman period. Alternatively the practices thus designated may have been part of the contemporary scene in remote areas or among people with less pretensions to modernity than the Roman littérateur.

In this discussion of food-plants we have only touched upon one aspect of the life of the agrarian poor in Roman Italy, and considered some of the literary evidence. Further study of the life of shepherds and peasant cultivators in the various regions of the peninsula in ancient times may well modify any conclusions which can be drawn at this stage. Moreover we have not attempted here to trace any chronological development. Change takes place very slowly in this sphere, but its pace and direction may be perceptible if comparison is made with the rural customs of later ages.

Notes to Chapter Four

1. Pliny, *N.H.* XIX passim.
2. cf. Pliny, *N.H.* XVI, I: 'Pomiferae arbores quaeque mitioribus sucis voluptatem primae cibis attulerunt et necessario alimento delicias miscere docuerunt.' (References to Pliny are to the Teubner edition).
3. *Plants and Archaeology* (1967), 31. The point is also made by D. and P. Brothwell, *Food in Antiquity* (1969), 115ff, where some Roman examples are given. This survey relies heavily upon Apicius, who, being an exponent of the *haute cuisine* of the Empire, is difficult to handle as evidence for earlier periods or different social classes.
4. This attitude to the forest is also observable in the history of the Italian *selva*, as for example in Dante, *Inferno* I, 2 and throughout the poem, where it is a place of wandering and confusion. Owing to deforestation the modern Italian countryman is more likely to regard *la montagna* as the wilderness.
5. Varro, *Res Rusticae* I, 45.
6. Pliny, *N.H.* XX, 19 (77).
7. *Agrestis* is also used to mean 'wild', though not by Cato and only in one paragraph by Varro. This is III, 7, in reference to pigeons and even here the connection with *agri* is strong. It may also have this sense in II, 1, 4, where it is combined with *ferus*, perhaps to confirm the meaning. Theophrastus distinguishes another type of plant which he describes as οπώηδ. This is usually translated as 'herbaceous', in the sense of the Italian *erbaceo* as defined by E. Baroni, *Guida*

Botanica d'Italia ed. S. B. Zanetti (1955) 695: 'Verde o della consistenza molle dell' erba, in opposizione a colorato o legnoso'.

8. Plautus, *Pseudolus*, I, 825. The point is made even more clearly in I, 811, when he speaks of other cooks 'qui mihi condita prata in patinis proferunt'.

9. *De Re Rustica* XI, 3, 54. (ed. Lundström, 1906).

10. *De Agri Cultura* VI, 3. (ed. A. Mazzarino, 1962).

11. Pliny *N.H.* XIX, 4 (19) 'Silvestres fecerat natura corrudas ut passim quisque demeteret: ecce altiles spectantur asparagi . . .'

12. *N.H.* XIX, 8 (42).

13. For a similar practice in later times, see *Culpeper's Complete Herbal* (repr. 1970), 33: (Asparagus Sativus) 'It groweth usually in gardens, and some of it grows wild in Appleton Meadows, in Gloucestershire, where the poor people do gather the buds of young shoots, and sell them cheaper than our garden asparagus is sold in London'.

14. *De Re Rustica* XI, 3, 37.

15. cf. Columella, *De Arboribus* XXV, 1, 'Amygdala si parum feracia erunt, perforata arbore lapidem adigito: ita librum arboris inolescere sinito'. Also Theophrastus, *Hist. Plant.* II, 4, 3.

16. cf. Pliny, *N.H.* XIX, 30 (94).

17. For another example of *transferre*, where it may have the meaning 'move from the wild to cultivation', see Pliny, XIX, 54 (170) where in reference to mustard (*sinapi*) he says it grows 'nulla cultura, melius tamen planta tralata'. cf. XIX, 29 (92): 'siser transferre melius', where he has not mentioned sowing it, and has just been writing about elecampane (*inula*) being propagated 'oculis ex radice excisis'.

18. *N.H.* XIX, 55 (172).

19. *De Re Rustica* XI, 3, 39 (ed. A. Josephson, 1955).

20. *De Re Rustica*, IX, 4, 4.

21. cf. a much later example, this time from pasture-land in *Travels in the Two Sicilies*, 1777-80, by Henry Swinburne, London, 1783-1785, Vol. I, 227: 'Our next stage was to Manfredonia, twenty miles through a flat pasture covered with asphodels, thistles, wild artichokes, and fennel-giant; of the last are made bee-hives and chair-bottoms; the leaves are given to asses by way of a strengthener, and the tender buds are boiled and eaten as a delicacy by the peasants . . . The artichokes are given to buffaloes.'

22. E. Isaac, *The Geography of Domestication* (1970), 114.

23. *Marcelli de Medicamentis*, ed. G. Helmreich, 1889.

24. *Prehistoric Europe: The Economic Basis* (1952) 115.

25. *Histoire de l'alimentation végétale depuis la préhistoire jusqu'à nos jours*, trans. F. Guidon (1932), 608-28.

26. *The Early Growth of the European Economy* (1974), 16-17, cf. idem, *Rural Economy and Country Life in the Medieval West* (1968), 9 and 21-22.

27. Theophrastus, *Hist. Plant.* VII, 6, 1; G. W. Dimbleby, op. cit. (note 3), 31, *et al.*

28. Περὶ λεπτυνούσης διαίτης (ed. Nino Marinone, *La Dieta dimagrante*, Torino, 1973), 9, 72 (p. 86). Galen does make an exception in favour of γογγυλίδες and βολβοί. On the latter Marinone has an interesting comment: 'I suoi bulbi (non le radici, come ritiene Galeno) sono mangerecci e constituiscono un cibo noto ancor oggi nell'Italia meridionale con il nome di lampascioni'.

29. *De Alimentorum Facultatibus*, XLII (p. 628, Teubner edition, 1965) 'διαφέρει δὲ τῶν ὁμοειδῶν φυτῶν ξηρότητι μὲν τὸ ἄγριον, ὑγρότητι δὲ τὸ κηπευόμενον.'

30. *De Alimentorum Facultatibus* II, 64.

31. The *moretum* has often been described as a cake, most recently by Bertha Tilly in a note to Varro, *R.R.* I, 13, 2, in *Varro the Farmer* (1973), 166. The ingredients mentioned in the *Moretum* of the *Appendix Vergiliana* (cf. Columella, XII, 59) produce a mixture of softer consistency than a cake, unless a disproportionate amount of cheese is used. This might sometimes have been done, and the product would have been a herb-flavoured cheese. But cheese was not an essential ingredient of the *moretum*, as may be seen from Columella, XII, 59, where two of the recipes given omit the cheese. Although the use of the word *globus* in 1. 117 suggests a cake, the *moretum* of the *Appendix Vergiliana* is to be eaten as a relish with bread. It forms a *globus* when it is being mixed and the fragments are gathered in from the edges (cf. the use of *conglobari* in reference to similar processes). The mention of *aioli* by D. and P. Brothwell, op. cit. (note 3), 109, also has some bearing upon this question.

32. *N.H.* XX, 24-6.

33. *N.H.* XX, 26 (64).

34. These, as we are reminded by R. MacMullen in *Enemies of the Roman Order* (1966), 253, must have occurred frequently in the ancient world. In the anecdote from Galen to which he refers, the peasants suffered not because they were eating wild foods, but because they were forced by famine to do so indiscriminately. For remarks upon the incidence of famine, see C. Clark and M. Haswell, *The Economics of Subsistence Agriculture* (1967), 60.

CHAPTER FIVE

The Effects of Social and Political Change upon the Small Farmer

For many smallholders in ancient Italy, living in farmsteads remote from the centres of political power, events which appeared momentous to their urban contemporaries must have passed almost unnoticed. Certain developments, however, in the social and political life of Rome and later of Italy as a whole must have had an even greater impact upon the countryman than upon the town-dweller. Amid the profusion of material available attention will be directed to a few examples which seem likely to be particularly useful when studied in this way. The period in which the largest proportion of the population of Rome itself was engaged in farming at subsistence level must have occurred immediately after the foundation of the first settlement there. Unfortunately for our present purpose there remains, and may always remain, a considerable measure of uncertainty about the events and chronology of Rome's first three centuries. During this period the amount of open land within the walls and near neighbourhood of the city must gradually have decreased owing to the construction of buildings and roads. In the *Twelve Tables*, 449 BC, there is already some evidence of what, to a contemporary, might well have seemed an overcrowding of the city and its *ager*.[1] No doubt these laws could be applied to other situations later,[2] but it is of particular interest here to consider in what context their provisions first arose.

When Pliny (*N.H.* XVI, 6 (15)) refers to a statement about *glandes* in the *Twelve Tables*, he is using the word as in the rest of the paragraph to mean the fruits of the oak or the beech. Acorns and beech-mast were valuable pig-food, and the right to pick them up was of great importance at a time when pig-rearing was the poor man's only chance of a meat supply. In the *Twelve Tables* VII, 7 (ROL p. 470) we encounter the question of road-making. It is often thought that the permission 'to drive beasts where he wishes' refers to driving a herd of cattle or a flock of sheep. But both Festus (564, 1) and Cicero, *Pro Caecina* XIX, 54, refer specifically to *iumentum*, a beast of burden. Moreover Cicero uses it in the singular. It is probable that when this provision was put into the *XII Tables* it referred to the leading or driving[3] of a mule along a 'road' which passed or crossed many land-holdings of various sizes and types. Such mule-tracks today cover many miles and are usually paved with stones. If they have fallen into disrepair or the stones have been removed, it is difficult in winter and early spring for man or beast to gain a foothold, and the path becomes a morass. The only expedient is to strike out through the adjacent land wherever it is firm and comparatively dry. This seems to have been what Roman law originally allowed one to do.

In these early laws problems of town and country appear side by side, reminding us of their close connection. R. M. Ogilvie (in *Commentary on Livy, Books I-V*, p. 294), with reference to Livy's account of the events of 495 BC, draws a distinction between farm-labourers and 'the petty craftsmen and traders and workers' living in the city at this time. It is possible, however, that as yet such a clear distinction did not usually exist between those who plied a trade and those who tilled the land. The vintner, the joiner, the oil-merchant and the baker must all originally have developed their trades alongside their farming pursuits. The close connection between the stock-in-trade of such 'industries' and the produce of the farm suggests that these traders would have been slow to relinquish their agricultural activities or those of their families.[4]

The provisions of the *XII Tables* confirm the impression we gain from Livy II (chapters 23, 27, *et passim*) that the lending of money in some form and the charging of interest on it was well-established in Rome in the fifth century BC, and that under certain conditions[5] a debtor might be imprisoned or even enslaved by his creditor. While treating with due caution the chronology and details of the first five books of Livy's history, it will be worth while for us to glance at his account of the plebeians' struggle against debt-bondage or *nexum*. Livy's narrative is no doubt coloured by the fact that debt was always a menace to the small farmer right up to his own time, and that class warfare continued. But were the protagonists in this story really the rural (or even the urban) poor? The poor are remarkably elusive in Roman literature, especially in prose.

To take one example, from Livy II, 23, the old centurion rushes into the forum to appeal for the sympathy of his fellow citizens. If for the moment we accept this story in the form in which we find it, several points of interest arise from it. Whatever may have been this man's condition as a bondsman, he did not belong to the *capite censi*, for he had been serving in the army and he paid *tributum*. Moreover he had owned *pecora*. He was not one of those who lived 'in casis ritu pastorum agrestiumque' (Livy V, 53, 5). He did not live in a *tugurium* like L. Quinctius Cincinnatus (Livy III, 26, 11-12) but in a *villa*. Used of a dwelling in this early period *villa* does not signify anything elaborate, but taken with the other indications here it suggests the steading of a fairly prosperous yeoman farmer. This is not the peasant at subsistence level, growing a minimum of grain, searching for vegetable foods, and keeping at best a few pigs or grazing some sheep on the common pasture. While we have no means of knowing how authentic Livy's mise en scène here is, this passage is one which should make us consider carefully what class of person was chiefly involved in the early financial and agrarian disputes.

Livy has identified debt as one of the chief problems of fifth-century Rome, and Plutarch suggests, as we might also infer from Livy's story discussed above, that it did not only affect the very poor, but also τοὺς - - - - - - κεκτημένους μέτρια.' (Plutarch, *Coriolanus* V, 2). It may be objected that these authors are reading back into the fifth century BC the problems they knew to exist in later times. If the very poor were involved in debt, it could only have been because of crop failures resulting in famine, and these are indeed reported by Livy for the same period. Any formal loan on which interest was payable would have been rare in these circumstances: the farmer or miller rather than the *faenerator* would have been the lender. The only situation in which one would expect a third party to have been involved would have arisen if the grain had to be obtained from outside the *territorium* of Rome. Men in more comfortable circumstances might incur debt because of large taxes, buying or renting of land, renting summer pasture or purchasing animals for sacrifice. Since we have no certain information as to the type of citizen who was raising loans which he could not repay, or the reasons for which he needed them, we must approach the social problems of early Rome in another way.

The chief causes of friction in an expanding settlement would be shortage of cultivable land within reach of the city, and the change, at whatever stage it took place, from a system of barter and a subsistence economy to the use of metal (coined or uncoined) as a medium of exchange. Modern authorities assure us[6] that there was no Roman coinage as such until the third century BC. The bronze mentioned as a medium of exchange in the *XII Tables* must have been *aes rude* (Thomsen, op. cit. p. 259) or *aes signatum,* and in either case was weighed out to the required amount on any given occasion. If there is any truth in the annalists' picture of the misery caused by debt in the fifth century it may be connected with the wider use of bronze as a medium of exchange.[7] It could, however, merely reflect later economic problems, for example those arising in the second century BC. In the first four books of his history and indeed beyond these, Livy assumes that coined money is already in use, though in IV, 60, 6, he realises that as there was no silver coinage at that date a large sum of money would have had to be paid in the form of *aes grave*, not coins. When he writes of small sums being contributed as part of a public collection, thereby implying the use of coins, it is in an emotive context, as in II, 33, 11, and III, 18, 11, when the plebs contribute money for a public funeral as a mark of respect to a great man. There is a 'widow's mite' touch about these instances, and Livy is probably not intending to convey that the actual coins existed at that time. However, as Thomsen (*Early Roman Coinage*, Vol. III, p. 259) writes: 'There are a great many statements in Livy and other ancient authors referring to the use of bronze money in this period, and frequently it appears clearly from the wording that the authors themselves believed that proper coins were involved'. (The period to which he refers is the fifth century BC).

Before the introduction of a monetary system the small farmer, accustomed to borrow grain in time of scarcity from a more fortunate neighbour, would have repaid in kind at the next harvest.[8] Now he must pay in cash and with interest. The price of the borrowed grain would be fixed in the time of scarcity, not at the harvest. Under such conditions a peasant farmer is always at a disadvantage, as Pliny remarks (*Epist.* III, 19) in a specific instance concerning rented land: 'The last owner on more than one occasion sold up the tenants' possessions, so that he temporarily reduced their arrears but weakened their resources for the future, and consequently their debts mounted up again' (trans. B. Radice, Penguin Classics). He cannot realise his assets without losing his livelihood, and, if living at subsistence level, with no margin, he has no means of escape. It is unlikely that the subsistence farmer in the early Republic would have handled much money at all, because he would not be involved in many cash transactions. It is thought that even in the classical period the farmer did not possess much currency. (M. H. Crawford, JRS, 60 (1970) p. 44). Even in reference to the Imperial age, R. Duncan-Jones (*The Economy of the Roman Empire*, p. 7) says: 'Surviving coin-hoards come most often from well-to-do households and need not indicate widespread peasant ownership of money . . . Nevertheless it remains possible on general grounds that money was less pervasive in the countryside than in the towns'. Martial was familiar with the penniless condition of the farmer in his own day:

'Ebrius et crudus nil habet agricola'.

'The farmer has no money, but plenty to eat and drink' (XII, 76). So was Horace, who (in *Odes* I, 1, 17-18) wrote of the merchant giving up his overseas trading ventures after a bad passage for the safer life of the countryside.

'mox reficit rates
quassas indocilis pauperiem pati.'

At the time when Rome was turning to a money economy the population was increasing and buildings and cultivation were gradually occupying all the available land in and around the city. In earlier times the settler who needed more land had only to clear another patch of the forest and use it,[9] but Appian (*Civil Wars*, I, 1, 7) remarks on the inequalities which arose from this situation. What Livy (XXXIX, 54) describes as happening in Gaul in 183 BC, 'exposuerunt se superante in Gallia multitudine inopia coactos agri et egestate ad quaerendam sedem Alpes transgressos, quae inculta per solitudines viderent, ibi sine ullius iniuria consedisse,' had happened in Italy also, even in the vicinity of Rome itself. But as the city grew, the cultivated land in and beyond the *ager Romanus* was occupied, and there were few chances of extending one's holding unofficially in that area. In the fourth and fifth centuries BC the struggle for land was for holdings near enough to Rome for purposes of trade and political activity, safety and ease of communications.[10] In Livy III, 1, 4-6 we are told that when the colony was founded at Antium there were not enough Romans willing to go there, and the number had to be made up with Volsci. 'cetera multitudo poscere Romae agrum malle quam alibi accipere' (Livy III, 1, 6). Later there was a struggle for land near any town or main route for the same reasons. It is against this background that we should read the early history of Rome as our literary sources offer it to us. In so far as the amount of land available to Roman citizens increased with the growth of population during the fifth and fourth centuries BC it did so by conquest and the formation of colonies (P. A. Brunt, *Italian Manpower*,

Table II, p. 30). Brunt thinks that the land which became *ager publicus* at this time was probably already being exploited by the governing class at Rome, and that the great estates may already have been in the process of formation.[11] At any rate by 366 BC when the Lex Licinia Sextia was introduced there must have been need to adjust the balance of land tenure in favour of the less wealthy owners. The law in the form in which it has come down to us[12] was not a very radical measure, and can have been intended only to deal with a specific problem. To keep the matter in proportion we must remember that there were at least nineteen agrarian laws before this.[13] Many of these dealt only with the allocation of a particular area of newly-conquered territory, but together they show that the possession of land was already a very lively issue, and that the Senate expected to control the distribution at least of new territory.[14]

During the Samnite Wars and the war with Pyrrhus many farmers would have had to leave their farms to join the army, but this would not usually have affected the smallholders. The property qualification for entering the army was originally 11,000 *asses*, subsequently lowered in the middle of the second century BC to 4,000 (Polybius, VI, 19, 2). Brunt (*Social Conflicts in the Roman Empire*, p. 29) estimates that in the second century this sum of 4,000 *asses* could not have represented more than 'a cottage, garden, and some personal belongings'. If this was so, the owner of property worth only 1,500 *asses* must have had a very meagre living and the *incensi* were destitute indeed. The limit was probably not reduced to 1,500 *asses*, its lowest figure, until sometime between 133 BC and 107 BC.[15] The very poor were only called up when a *tumultus* occurred and there was a *tumultuarius dilectus*. This (Gabba, op. cit., p. 181) first occurred in 380-1 BC. The Romans were chary of such general calls to arms for reasons expressed by Valerius Maximus (II, 3) who says that the *populus* (which evidently means here the relatively affluent members of it) were eager to undertake the hardships of military service so that the general would not have to call up the poor and give them weapons. The *inopia* of the *proletarii* made people uneasy about having them in the army. This is supported by Gellius, who says

(XVI, 10, 11) that the poor were only called up 'in tumultu maximo'.

During the Punic Wars, however, especially when Hannibal was in Italy, every man of military age was needed and even the *proletarii* were called up. In early times when the term of service lasted only six months or one campaigning season, it would not have caused great hardship to a farmer, but when they were kept with their legions for several years, the effect upon their farms might be ruinous.[16] Brunt (*Italian Manpower*, p. 400) gives the average length of service in the Hannibalic War as seven years. He adds: 'It is significant that not only Scipio's veterans but the legionaries who had been in Sardinia received compensation in the form of land allotments at the end of the war; presumably their farms had been ruined during their absence for 13, 9, or merely 7 years'. An additional hazard for the farmer in this war was the long occupation of southern Italy by Hannibal's troops, who were perforce living off the country. Again the matter must not be exaggerated. His retreat from the vicinity of Rome and Latium was rapid, though he stayed longer in South Italy. The poorest and most inaccessible plots would be most likely to escape harm in these circumstances. Farms on or near main lines of communication would suffer most, and these in Roman Italy were the more valuable and commercially successful holdings. Again, the loss of crops such a cereals or legumes would be more easily sustained, for they could be sown again. And in fact they were, for there are accounts of grain being collected from areas already devastated. In Livy XXIV, 14, we are told how the neighbourhood of Beneventum was devastated in 214 BC. In XXV, 13, Hanno is collecting the previous summer's grain from this same area, while in the fields the next crop (212 BC) is just appearing.

Where olives were destroyed the damage would be much more serious. This would not occur through foraging but in punitive raids, for example by the Romans upon *socii* who went over to Hannibal. The most severe losses would be sustained by the owners of properties of moderate size growing for the market. Owners of large properties had sufficient capital to weather the storm, and probably estates elsewhere. The very poor had not enough to be useful or noticeable and were in any case accustomed to periodic famines. Some parts of Italy, such as Bruttium, were affected more permanently by the war: Campania appears to have made a complete recovery, doubtless because of its fertility and its excellent climate. A market gardener today in the plain south of Salerno can count on three cash crops of vegetables per annum, and in Strabo's time:

'ἱστορεῖται δ'ἔνια τῶν πεδίων σπείρεσθαι δι'ἔτους δίς μὲν τῇ ζειᾷ, τὸ δὲ τρίτον ἐλύμῳ, τινὰ δὲ καὶ λαχανεύεσθαι τῷ τετάρτῳ σπόρῳ.'[17].

The effect of the devastation would vary with the type of country and the nature and size of the farm. Moreover this ravaging of the countryside was not a new phenomenon in the Hannibalic War. It had long been the regular method of warfare in Italy between Rome and her enemies, if we are to believe Livy (V, 24; VI, 31; VII, 22 and IX, 20). Clerici[18] accepts this, and even considers (p. 64) that the frequent occurrence of such devastation delayed the spread of the cultivation of the olive and the vine into Latium, where they only became a major part of Roman agriculture in the second half of the fourth century BC.[19]

The agrarian law of Tiberius Gracchus, 133 BC, has often been closely associated with the effect upon agriculture of the Second Punic War. H. C. Boren[20] thinks otherwise. He suggests that Tiberius Gracchus was attempting to deal with an urban crisis which had developed owing to the cessation of state building programmes and government spending in general just before 133 BC. The movement of peasant farmers to Rome would in this case have been voluntary, owing to the attractions of city life in a period of plenty. Even this theory has its connections with the Punic Wars, as they were partially responsible, in terms of plunder and indemnities for the increase in wealth in Rome during the early part of the second century. In support of the more conventional view we have the moving account of Plutarch (*Tiberius Gracchus*, VIII 7) of Tiberius Gracchus travelling through Etruria on his way to Numantia and finding the country deserted except for slave labourers.[21] Before our sympathy is too deeply engaged, we must remember that Plutarch ascribes this story to τινι βιβλίῳ of Caius Gracchus. It is a piece of political propaganda and is clearly presented as such by Plutarch. Even when this is admitted the purpose of the Lex Sempronia is still obscure. D. C. Earl (*Tiberius Gracchus: A Study in Politics*, p. 18)[22] says that the only assertion which can safely be made about the Lex Sempronia is that it restricted existing *possessores* of *ager publicus* to a maximum holding of 500 *iugera* and possibly they were also allowed to retain an additional 250 for each child. He rejects the translation of Appian's παῖδες as 'sons'. The same writer concludes that the allotments for the poor were nearer ten *iugera* than thirty, and that only Roman citizens were to benefit, not the allies.[23] He infers from Livy XXVIII, 11, 8-11 (p. 25) that even in 133 BC Northern Italy consisted largely of farms of smaller size than 500 *iugera*, on public land at least. The passage may be said to suggest this, but only two towns in Northern Italy are mentioned, Cremona and Placentia. It does prove that the land allocated to settlers in these two colonies was still owned by a considerable number of peasant farmers, who were now being recalled to continue their work there. The peremptory manner in which according to Livy's account these citizens were forced to return to the land[24] already seems to foreshadow the Byzantine peasant's life-long bondage to the soil.

Earl then goes on to calculate the extent to which he thinks *ager publicus* was held in excess of five hundred *iugera*, suggesting that as the census figures for 125-4 show an increase of 76,000 over those of 131-0, this represents the men settled on Gracchan allotments. It is difficult, however, to base an exact calculation on these figures.[25] If the Gracchan distribution did have this effect upon the census of 125-4 it would seem to have been carried out with remarkable speed. This may also be evidenced by the boundary marks found.[26] Though these are too few to give any impression of the extent of the enterprise, they are interesting in that they mostly come from South Italy (Campania, Lucania, Apulia). These *termini* may only indicate preparation for a settlement and a preliminary survey. In view of what Cicero had to say later, in *De Lege Agraria*, 81-4, about settling colonists in Campania, it is not surprising that the work of the land commissioners was controversial. But these areas contained much land which had been confiscated from the *socii* after the war with Hannibal and were therefore more suitable than might otherwise appear.

The theory which Earl advances with regard to the Lex Sempronia is that it was not a measure to relieve poverty or to improve the agricultural situation, but a legal device to secure an increase in the number of citizens qualified by the amount of their property to serve in the army.[27] This would also account for the speed with which the measure was implemented. Brunt (in a review of Earl, op. cit., in *Gnomon*, XXXVII (1965) p. 189) agrees that there was a shortage of *assidui* but asks: 'how could this shortage have come about except by the concentration of land in fewer hands and the impoverishment of the peasantry? And how could this process fail to bring about a social crisis?' E. Badian,[28] while he considers that a social and economic crisis did face Rome at this time, regards it as 'at every step, linked with, and overshadowed by, a military crisis, which was assuming an increasingly alarming aspect'. The reference here is to the military defeats in Spain and the slave risings in Italy and Sicily. The task of the Gracchan land commissioners, except in relation to land recently acquired by the state, was extremely complicated. This appears very clearly in Appian's account,[29] where he writes of the difficulty of discovering titles to lands when farmers had cultivated the ἀνέμητος land at random. Since the time when the Lex Licinia Sextia was passed, land had been lost and recaptured in war, estates divided or joined, owners had been killed in the Punic Wars and the legal status of whole towns had changed. A task which had been comparatively simple in 367 and before must have been so complicated in 133 as to afford every encouragement to Tiberius' opponents. This type of land law was already an anachronism.

If the Lex Sempronia only concerned Roman citizens it would not have affected the majority of the rural population of Italy at all, unless they had large holdings of Roman *ager publicus* or were non-Romans displaced from their farms by the new settlers. The question of displacing the *socii* from their holdings may well have caused Gaius Gracchus to experiment with planting a colony abroad — if indeed his settlement at Carthage was the first official colony overseas (Velleius, I, 15, 4). But these colonists were drawn from the χαριεστάτοι τῶν πολιτῶν.[30] and they were allocated 200 *iugera* each — enough to form the basis of a sound commercial enterprise if capital was available to staff and equip it. They therefore lie somewhat outside the scope of our present study. According to Plutarch (*Gaius Gracchus*, 9) Gaius Gracchus was opposed by Livius Drusus who was offering colonial land to the ἄποροι.[31] Brunt (Italian Manpower, p. 217) mentions other kinds of agricultural settlements abroad which can be attributed to this period, but which were unofficial. He considers that Julius Caesar was the first to organise overseas colonisation on a large scale.

As to the extent to which the Lex Sempronia benefited the landless citizens and slowed down the depopulation of the countryside, there are differences of opinion. Gabba (*Motivazioni economiche*, p. 134) regards the law as anachronistic and considers that even if the small peasant farm had been re-established, it would have met again the same difficulties which caused its decline in the first half of the second century BC: agriculture was becoming more specialised and needed larger units. This development he traces to the extension of Rome's power overseas and the increasing use of imported foodstuffs. Whether this trade was sufficiently far-reaching in the late second century to affect radically the agricultural pattern throughout the peninsula is uncertain. It would seem that depopulation was at this time not an urgent problem except in certain areas (Brunt, *Italian Manpower*, p. 77) for particular local reasons, and Gabba himself admits that the small peasant holding 'nella realtà dell' agricoltura italica è ben testimoniata ancora nel I sec. a.C.' (p. 138). At least some of the Gracchan settlers must have made a genuine attempt to farm their allotments of land and to be self-supporting in the countryside, though if the bill was primarily introduced for military or administrative reasons, this would not officially have been important. What we can conclude with certainty from these events, as from many other instances, is that the better land in Italy was very frequently changing hands during the last two centuries of the Republic. This in itself was a disadvantage for agricultural progress and may have led to the neglect of long-term projects such as drainage and irrigation. The growth of the *latifundia,* which does not manifest itself prominently before the end of the Republic, though it evidences the gradual disappearance of the medium-sized farm (owner-occupied), meant a measure of stability for the countryside which it had previously lacked. However none of this affected the dwellers on the marginal plots in marshy or mountainous country. They continued to scrape a meagre living from the soil as they had always done.

Notes to Chapter Five

1. In Table VII, sections 1-6 seem to be concerned with problems arising from the proximity to one another of buildings and plots of land. Some of the provisions relate to very small distances, more appropriate to village or small-town growth than to estates or buildings in open country, e.g. VII, 3, ROL, p. 46-48.
2. As Cicero suggests for laws of all kinds in *Pro Caecina,* 18-19.
3. For *agere* with *iumenta* see Livy I, 48, 5, but there the animals are drawing a carriage.
4. In CEHE, Vol. I, p. 122, the reverse process is shown to be taking place in the third century AD. Towns are declining and farmers are once again having to supply as many as possible of their own needs.
5. Table III, 1-6, ROL, p. 436-8.
6. R. Thomsen, *Early Roman Coinage,* Vol. III, p. 257 and H. Zehnacker, *Moneta,* p. 198.
7. The Roman plebs could have been in debt to Etruscans who were using local agents, as the Roman money-lenders are said to have done in 193 BC (Livy XXXV, 7) in Latium.
8. It is interesting to note that in a Sicilian village in 1929 debts were paid immediately after the harvest. See *Milocca, A Sicilian Village,* C. G. Chapman, p. 23, and on p. 143: 'These payments, like all others, are made at harvest time'. Compare the remark of E. E. Huggett regarding the European peasantry of the seventeenth century (*The Land Question,* p. 30): 'the peak of credit was reached in the spring after the difficulties of the winter, falling off considerably in autumn after a successful harvest.'
9. In less populous areas this situation continued much longer. cf. E. Boserup, *The Conditions of Agricultural Growth,* p. 57: 'Never-

theless, most of Europe seems to have been cultivated by the system of fire, axe and forest fallow as late as the time of the Roman Empire . . .'

10. In Livy VIII, 11, 6, there is an indication of this, when land is being distributed, 'bina in Latino iugera . . .terna in Falerno quadrantibus etiam pro longinquitate adiectis.'

11. At the same time, the good land in convenient areas being now fully occupied, the quality of land available was poor, and this meant lower yields and a harder struggle for livelihood for those occupying it. The contrast between those with large holdings of good land and the rest was therefore inevitably becoming more conspicuous. See also Livy's account of the *trientabulum* (XXXI, 13, 5-9). Land offered in 200 BC in part-payment of the debt to the citizens was situated 'intra quinquagesimum lapidem'. From this phrase Livy intends his readers to conclude that the land was desirable and valuable.

12. Livy, VI, 35, 4; X, 13, 15; Varro, R. R., I, 29., *et al.*

13. See Clerici, *Economia e Finanza dei Romani*, p. 302, note 1, for the list.

14. For a different view see G. Tibiletti, *Ricerche di Storia agraria romana*, Athenaeum, vol. XXVIII, 1950, p. 239, where he concludes that agrarian policy in the sixty years preceding the Gracchi was 'larga, conciliante e tollerante' and did not cause much excitement.

15. E. Gabba, *Athenaeum* XXVII (1949), p. 174. He thinks a more precise date impossible.

16. As our literary sources suggest, e.g. Livy XXV, 1, 8.

17. Strabo, V, 4, 3.

18. Clerici, *Economia e Finanza dei Romani*, p. 63.

19. Clerici, op cit., p. 90, note 14.

20. *The Urban Side of the Gracchan Economic Crisis*, Ancient History Review, 63 (1957-8), p. 890-902.

21. If we compare this with Livy XXVIII, 11, 6, it will be noted that Livy adds that there was a shortage of slaves.

22. *Tiberius Gracchus: A Study in Politics*, Coll. Latomus, vol. LXVI, p. 18.

23. E. Badian, *Tiberius Gracchus and the beginning of the Roman Revolution*, Aufstieg und Niedergang der Römischen Welt, Vol. 1, 1972, Berlin, p. 704, notes that thirty *iugera* is probably the limit of the Gracchan assignments, but he writes: 'it is only a maximum: we have no clue as to the mean or median size'.

24. Livy, XXVIII, 11, 8.

25. Brunt, *Italian Manpower*, p. 70-71, discusses the census returns
26. Degrassi, ILLR, Vol. I, p. 269.
for 168-124 BC.

27. E. Gabba, *Motivazioni economiche nell'Opposizione alla Legge di Tib. Sempronio Gracco*, in *Polis and Imperium*, Studies in honour of E. T. Salmon, Toronto, 1974, also adopts this view: 'Tib. Gracco era preoccupato dal vedere un declino delle capacità militari romane e cercava di porvi rimedio. E poichè aveva identificato le cause del declino nel venir meno della classe contadina, cercava di ricostituirla'. (p. 129).
28. Badian, *Tiberius Gracchus and the beginning of the Roman Revolution*, p. 687.
29. Appian, *Civil Wars*, I, 7, 26-29.
30. Plutarch, *Caius Gracchus* IX, 2.
31. If it is true that Livius was trying to 'undercut' C. Gracchus like this, it suggests that even the younger Gracchus was not dealing with the poorest citizens. cf. E. T. Salmon, *Roman Colonization,* p. 120-1.

CHAPTER SIX

Colonies and Centuriation

Many of the smallholders in Roman Italy must have farmed the plots of land which formed part of the centuriation grids and as such are often still visible today. Attention was drawn to these systems by the publication in 1957 of J. S. P. Bradford's *Ancient Landscapes* and they are now well known. Some method of apportionment of land in the neighbourhood of towns may have existed before the introduction of regular centuriation. The tradition of the citizen's *heredium* of two *iugera*, if it can be ascribed to an early date, would suggest this in the case of Rome itself, as also would the emphasis upon boundaries in the XII Tables. Mention of the five-foot strip to be left between two plots (Table VII) implies exact measurement. F. T. Hinrichs (*Die Geschichte der gromatischen Institutionen*, pp. 38-48) has noted indications in the position of roads and field boundaries today of what he regards as a form of land allocation preceding full Roman centuriation, and identifies this with the division into *strigae* and *scamna* mentioned in the *Libri Coloniarum*.[1] Examples given include certain tracts of countryside near Alatri, Nepi, Rieti, Venafro and Falerii Novi. While there are many difficulties in attempting to trace detailed plans of land assignment datable to the fourth and fifth centuries BC, the existence of some organised pattern of allocations in Central Italy in this early period is not in itself improbable. Greek cities in South Italy and Sicily were laid out according to a rectilinear plan at least as early as the sixth century BC and land outside the city walls could be treated in the same way.² The need for this system arose for the Greeks from their position as colonists. Any such division of land applied to Roman or other territory in Central Italy must in the first instance have arisen from the pressure of a settled agricultural population upon the resources of a limited area. We should therefore expect it to occur, if at all, when the increase of population and growth of urban settlements had severely limited opportunities of opening up new land. These conditions would have applied to parts of Latium and Southern Etruria, as well as the immediate environs of Rome, in the fourth century BC, or even earlier. Most authorities date the beginning of the Roman use of regular centuriation to the late fourth century BC,³ but the traditional *heredium* of two *iugera* of land for every citizen is attributed by our literary sources to Romulus.⁴ Such a wide discrepancy merits some consideration even though it concerns a proto-historical period. Allocations of heritable land could have been made to Roman citizens at an early date on the basis of less exact scales of measurement or scales differing from those of the classical *limitatio*, and there are indeed examples of different standards, as at Cosa and Alba Fucens.⁵ Mention of the two *iugera*, however, seems to associate the *heredium* with regular centuriation rather than with any preceding assignments. There is, of course, the possibility that the plot of two *iugera* was thought to have been the original allocation simply because it was the smallest unit of the existing system, and the tradition grew from this. Alternatively we may ask whether it is more probable that the *heredium* as a legal concept belongs to the fourth or fifth century BC than to the regal period or the early years of the Republic. Classical authors lacked a firm chronological basis for events before 390 BC⁶ and mention of Romulus indicates the venerable nature of an institution rather than its comparative dating. While bearing in mind these uncertainties regarding the establishment of the two *iugera* as the citizen's *heredium*, we shall consider the significance of the actual amount both to the citizen at home and to the colonist.

The earliest Roman, or Roman/Latin colonies, were founded according to tradition in the fifth century BC, but of these we have few details. Their positions suggest that they were planted primarily for strategic reasons.[7] Their name, however, of *coloniae* clearly implies farming activities. Though effective in guarding Latium and its approaches, they do not represent a significant change in the land use of Italy as a whole. If the tradition of the two *iugera* land allocation in colonies goes back to these earliest examples, the members of these colonies certainly fall into the category of smallholder we are discussing. Later colonies involved distributions of land in amounts ranging from two *iugera* to two hundred or more. The smallest and largest allocations both raise problems.

As has often been remarked, two *iugera* of land would be insufficient to support a family even at subsistence level. Estimates have been made as to the amount of land required for subsistence, but the figures given have to be treated with caution in relation to ancient farms, because the use of modern fertilisers and machinery may affect the crop yields, though this is less likely to occur in remote places and on small plots unsuited to mechanical aids. There is also in some instances a difference in the standard of living acceptable to a family at the present day. The difficulties involved in making estimates are indicated by the *Agricultural Policy Report* of the OECD entitled *Low Incomes in Agriculture* (Paris, 1964). On page 20, section 13, we read: 'In general, no precise criteria have been adopted to determine what constitutes a low farm income . . .' The report continues (p. 16): 'The opinions of farmers themselves as to what constitutes a low income naturally vary quite widely. In general, those who live in remote parts of the country may be satisfied with a lower standard of living than those who have more opportunities for comparison with people in other occupations; also, their costs of living may be lower'. The figures given in this report for farm sizes in Italy

give us a useful standard of comparison when we are considering
for example ancient allocations of 2, 5 or 6 *iugera*. On page 33
there is a table showing that in 1961 70 per cent of farms in Italy
were of less than 5 hectares. 12 per cent were between 5 and 10
hectares. Table 3, page 263, gives the proportion of farms of 1
hectare or less in 1961 as 33.1 per cent. The whole of this table
is of great interest in relation to the study of farm sizes in
antiquity. Recently the Cassa del Mezzogiorno has been distribut-
ing *poderi* (family-sized holdings) in Apulia-Lucania, and Franklin
(*The European Peasantry*, pp. 149-152) describes some of these.
They vary in size according to the amount of land available, some
falling below 1.5 ha (p. 148), others ranging from 2-4 ha, and
some being larger than this. In certain areas there is opportunity
for some members of the family to obtain other work, but this is
not universal, and in the past would seem to have been much
less likely than it is now. The Roman colonists at Vibo Valentia
(192 BC) received allocations of 15 *iugera*[8] and this would bring
them into the 2-4 ha category.

In the context of the peasant farmer's life in ancient Italy some
explanation can be offered for the existence of the two *iugera*
plots. If these, or any other very small allocations of land were
the norm during the regal period and immediately after it, they
formed part of the means of livelihood of a predominantly pastoral community. Any allocation of land to a family or to an
individual was therefore additional to the use of such pasture as
was locally available.[9] It was also additional to the use of wild
plants from the pasture or woodland or garigue. Even so, two
iugera would be insufficient for the production of a grain harvest
adequate to support a family whose staple diet was bread or
porridge.[10] In areas where the sweet chestnut was used for food
that would supply the deficiency. Pliny (*N.H.* XVI, 6 (15)) says
that acorns were used 'inopia frugum', but this probably refers
only to famine conditions, at least in historical times. Pliny is
including beech nuts under the general heading of *glandes*. An
explanation for the two *iugera heredium* has been put forward
by Westrup (*Introduction to Early Roman Law*, p. 47) who writes:
'The whole Greco-Roman tradition would seem to imply a certain

community of land as the original economic organisation of
Rome'. He thinks, however, that in countries such as Greece or
Italy the type of cultivation, involving plants of slow growth such
as the olive, led to a situation in which a family had long-term
use of a plot of land. From this in course of time developed a
system of private ownership. Westrup considers (p. 56) that in
early Rome land probably belonged to each *gens* as joint property.[11]
The individual family owned the flocks, but had only *possessio*,
the right of using the land. Each family, however, owned its house,
slaves and a small plot attached to the dwelling — the *heredium* or
hortus. This, according to Westrup's theory, was the only land
heritable, hence its name. If this view is accepted, there is no
problem as to how the family subsisted upon two *iugera*, because
they had the use of additional land.

We must also remember that food requirements as estimated
by modern European authorities often seem high in relation to
the actual diet of peoples in other areas and at other periods.
In *French Agriculture in the Seventeenth Century*,[12] Jean Jacquart
writes (p. 164): 'More than 75 per cent of French peasants in the
seventeenth century were cultivating insufficient land to provide
what today would be considered the bare essentials of life'. In
general the explanation of the two *iugera* plot for the early period
must lie in the pastoral activities of the farmer and his sale of
livestock, meat or dairy products. This implies some differentiation
of function at an early date, but is not unlikely, for example in
the sixth century BC in the neighbourhood of Rome. It is somewhat at variance with the tradition of an egalitarian distribution
of small plots to all citizens, but with the prosperous Etruscans
nearby, and with kings and nobles in their midst, Roman farmers
should have had little difficulty in disposing of surplus products
for barter, or later for cash. So much for those living within the
territorium of Rome. Those in remote places could have extended
their holding at will by clearing unoccupied land, even if it was of
poor quality and in scattered plots.[13] As we have seen, (pp. 65-6),
the later agrarian problems of the Romans arose chiefly as part of
the struggle for good land well situated, not simply for land itself.
It is possible that in early Rome the two *iugera* plot represented

the allocation of good, easily cultivable land in the *territorium* to be supplemented by marginal land of poor quality wherever it was available. One of the reasons for the increase in the size of allocations later may have been the fact that in that period extra land would have to be bought. These are attempts to provide a general explanation, but other factors may have been present in certain cases. Some members of a family may have worked for other landowners for part or all of the year. Some families may have been able to rent other land of good quality by private arrangement: this however would be less likely to occur when land values rose owing to scarcity, at any rate in the lower income groups.

In coastal colonies such as Tarracina, where according to Livy (VIII, 21, 6) the settlers received only two *iugera* each, it was possible for the colonists to supplement their income by fishing or trade. On the Adriatic coast the salt industry would provide a living.[14] Some coastal settlements, as often today, consisted of a village on the littoral and an associated community inland or on the cliffs. Braudel[15] considers the mixed economy of 'ploughed fields, market gardens, orchards, fishing and sea-going' to be very ancient. He writes of places where there is one village on the cliff and one below, and donkey traffic between the two. There is an example of this at Finale in Liguria, where the two original nuclei, dating back at least to medieval times, can still be identified. A similar type of mixed economy can be observed in some of the villages of the Cinque Terre.

The problem posed by the larger allocations of colonial land, which were usually associated with re-settlement of war veterans and sometimes involved larger allowances for higher ranks, is different. Allocations of 200 *iugera* were clearly adequate for subsistence, but could not be required for this alone. Moreover they presuppose some provision either by the colonist or by the authorities of money, equipment and labour. A farm of 240 *iugera*, for example, specialising in olive cultivation but with a flock of a hundred sheep, required according to Cato (*De Agri Cultura* X) a staff of thirteen, and Cato would not have erred on the side of extravagance.[16] Any form of mixed farming would seem likely to require a similar number of workers, if not more, for a holding of this size. Even supposing that the family of the *colonus* provided the work-force, and that he and they had the necessary skills, the money and the stock still had to be found to run the farm. These were the limiting factors which in many cases must account for the lack of volunteers to go out to a *colonia*. It is interesting to note that when a Latin colony was being planted at Castrum Frentinum (Livy, XXXV, 9, 7-8) and there were insufficient settlers, land allocations were not increased to use the vacant space. Livy himself remarks that the settlers could have been given more, but does not offer us any reason why this was not done.[17]

E. T. Salmon (*Roman Colonization under the Republic*, p. 120) is quite clear about the economic aspects of the large allocations, and he considers that even in the time Gaius Gracchus the equestrian order was involved: 'Some of Rome's paupers undoubtedly became landholders in the colonies at Tarentum and Scolacium. But even in these places the *coloni* also included men who were not paupers but who were interested in commerce, for which indeed both sites were well suited'. In reference to Carthago-Iunonia Salmon specifically remarks that allotments of two hundred *iugera* could hardly be worked except by a man with some capital. Moreover such enterprises could only be undertaken successfully in suitable localities where communications permitted widespread trading. In a situation where everyone had a plot of the same size, on the same type of land in the same district, local exchange of produce would be of little advantage. Salmon considers that Roman colonisation was not originally a measure of poor relief. but that its chief purpose was strategic (p. 15). Even after the Second Punic War: 'The colonies were intended to support a military programme, not to make provision for the needy' (p. 96). *Cicero* (*De Lege Agraria*, II, 73) certainly thought this was the aim.[18]

Roman authors do not give us many details of the way in which colonial land was worked or how the system affected the individual settler. This is probably because such matters were well-known and needed no explanation to their contemporaries. Grants of money to buy tools and stock may have been given.[19] Salmon (op. cit., p. 169, note 28) cites two examples which suggest that this might have been done, though neither concerns colonists in Italy. The first (Livy XL, 38) refers to the Ligures who were moved to Samnium and given money to help them settle into their new quarters. It should be noted that they were also allowed to take all their possessions with them. The other, from Appian (*Syr.* I) describes Antiochus providing colonists at Lysimachia with stock and equipment. Where the land was already under cultivation, as in the case of the Sullan confiscations, the equipment was probably taken over with the farm. In some cases, no doubt, the settler had possessed some little plot before and would transfer his portable property to the new holding. Cicero (*De Lege Agraria*, II, 79) did not seem to approve of this, but the fact that he mentions the idea and uses it as a debating point suggests that it was within the bounds of possibility. Sometimes the *colonus* seems to have engaged in commercial enterprise as well as, or instead of, his farming. Such trading activities at Anxur are mentioned with disapproval by Livy in V, 8, but this may only be because in this particular situation they led to disaster. In the fourth century BC when colonists set out in military fashion, marching under a banner to their *colonia*, they must at first have had with them military equipment, including items of more general use such as spades and baskets, and they must have carried rations. This is the more probable since the establishment of a colony in hostile territory often involved military operations. The transition from full-time soldier to full-time farmer would usually have been a slow process. At what date, if ever, Roman colonies ceased to be part of a military operation and began to be a civilian enterprise is not clear: Hinrichs (*Geschichte der gromatischen Institutionen*, p. 224) considers that the connection of civilian officials with the surveys dates from the appointment of special commissions to found the *coloniae maritimae* at the end of the war with the Latins in the fourth century BC. However, the commissioners continued to hold the *imperium* 'so that they could take any military measures necessary or override local authorities'. (Dilke, *Roman Land Surveyors*, p. 35). Colonies seem to have retained their military character much longer in the provinces, wherever strategy and security demanded.

We have in Virgil's *Eclogues* I and IX frequent references to farms changing owners, and to the taking over of land by Octavian's veterans. Although this is a poetical rather than a factual comment a few practical points seem to emerge. Meliboeus complains (I, 11ff) that he is being compelled to drive his goats away, because he has had to leave his farm. So in this case at any rate the incomer did not take over the stock. On the other hand line 71 suggests that he will reap the harvest. Virgil has seen fit to refer in these poems to the distress of the displaced farmer, which was familiar to him through his own experience or that of his contemporaries. Naturally we have no account in Roman literature of the feelings and experiences of the displaced Italian farmers who from time to time during the preceding centuries had given way to Roman or Latin colonists. Some of the land colonised may have been uninhabited at the time of appropriation, but much of it was in the hands of local Italian or Gallic peoples — the Samnites, Sabines, Marsi, Boii, to mention only a few.

The effects of Roman colonisation upon the poorer countryfolk of Italy were therefore twofold. Some of them, as Roman or Latin colonists, obtained small allocations of reasonably good land in the *territorium* of a town or stronghold. Others lost by the same process the land which they had farmed. The rest continued to cultivate their *paterna rura* as before. For we must not assume that even in the late Republic and early Empire there was no unallocated land in Italy. So impressive is the efficiency of the *agrimensores* and so widespread the traces of their work that we tend to forget the very specific purpose to which their efforts were directed. Centuriation was a method of solving an urban, not a rural problem. If the Romans were to have a garrison town or well-populated fortress in each colony, they had to face the same difficulty there as they had already encountered in urban Rome. Land must be found for the settlers as near as possible to their dwellings in the town. Moreover from the point of view of defence it was necessary to prevent the soldiery from being scattered over the countryside to cultivate outlying farms. That centuriation was essentially a town-based expedient can be seen from the manner in which it was carried out. Dilke[20] lists the positions in which the main intersection of the grid can be found. They are: at or near the central point of a settlement; on an existing road in it; or not far outside an existing or planned settlement. The centuriated area is at a point distant from the settlement (Dilke's category 4) chiefly in cases where mountains, rivers or other natural features have prevented centuriation in the immediate neighbourhood. The importance of the urban centre in this system is brought out even more clearly in the miniatures which illustrate the codices of the *gromatici*.[21] If these provide any evidence of the relative importance of the features of the land- scape, it was the town which mattered most. Some colonies were named after towns or cities already existing which the Romans had captured or received in surrender. In others the name of the colony soon became synonymous with that of the urban settle- ment which developed there. The effect of such an urbanised system can best be appreciated if it is compared with a method of cadastration based on village units, such as the Egyptian sys- tem described by D. J. Crawford.[22] These surveys differed from Roman centuriation in that they were applied, with local varia- tions, to the whole countryside, because they were made primarily for fiscal purposes. Centuriation registers could be used as a basis for taxation, but this does not seem to have been the primary object of the surveys.

Centuriation was not applied to all Roman land even in Italy. It affected chiefly *ager publicus* and therefore most of the terri- tory of the *coloniae*. Privately-owned land was not centuriated, though it might be surveyed and mapped upon occasion. The land which was assigned to colonists was distributed by lot from at least the time of the Gracchi, and the surveyor took the settlers, to their holdings in person and showed them the boundaries (Dilke, op. cit., p. 94). This indicates how important was the location of the plot and the quality of the land it comprised.[23] To obtain fair distribution, military precision was necessary, and the military nature of the operation would also encourage accept- ance of the allocation made. Many of the smallholders whom we are discussing must have received their allocations of land at the hands of an official surveyor, but many more did not. The least profitable land, and therefore that which was most likely to have been occupied by persons living at subsistence level, was wherever possible avoided by the land commissioners, or relegated to the category of *subseciva*. (cf. the illustration in Dilke, *The Roman Land Surveyors*, p. 101, of land near the river Pisaurus, which was labelled 'subseciva' because it was subject to flooding.) J. S. P. Bradford (*The Apulia Expedition: An Interim Report,* in *Antiquity,* 1950, p. 89) makes an interesting comment on some of the centuriated land in Apulia: 'The blank areas up to several miles wide between the systems, which were a puzzling feature on the photographs, were (we saw) caused by lower-lying ground which they did not choose to centuriate'. Sometimes part of the *ager* of a town was not centuriated, or not assigned, because there were insufficient colonists to occupy it. This is mentioned by Hyginus, *De Condicionibus Agrorum,* B 111-112,[24] who adds that sometimes the local non-Roman town was allowed to retain some of the land outside its walls.

In Agennius Urbicus, *De Controversiis Agrorum*[25] we read: 'Relicta sunt et multa loca, quae veteranis data non sunt'. This refers to land used as common pasture, but the writer continues (p. 47) with a description of the 'loca relicta', which consisted of mountainous country beyond the natural boundaries of a colony. Such land was usually annexed by the nearest tenants and was often the cause of controversies.[26] Upon the boundaries of the lands owned by Rome, and at any natural barrier which prevented further centuriation, there were patches of unsurveyed land described as *arcifinius.*[27] Then there were the *loca inculta* or *loca deserta,* which were among the terms used for land outside the official surveys. Such land did not always remain uncultivated, indeed it is often mentioned owing to a dispute about its cultivation or ownership.[28] It is usually represented in the illustrations on the centuriation diagrams as a mountain or range of mountains, and most of it was probably to be found in mountainous regions. Dilke[29] notes that some of the maps show high mountains where none exist. Is this because they are really *la montagna*[30] — the wilderness, that is, rough land uncenturiated?

Owing, however, to the conventions observed in these pictures, the 'wilderness' may sometimes appear deceptively small. These 'devia terrarum' included forests, marshes, saltings, and frontier lands throughout the peninsula, as well as those areas of the Apennines which were too high or too rocky to cultivate. 'Quod est tam asperum saxetum in quo agricolarum cultus non elaboret?' asks Cicero (*De Lege Agraria* II, 67), but he is probably concerned more with making a debating point than discussing agricultural conditions. The word *saxetum* is interesting. It seems as if Cicero may have coined it on analogy with *vinetum, olivetum* and *arbustum* or *arboretum*.[31] The idea conveyed is that of a cultivated patch where stones are the chief crop. Columella (II, 2, 12) advises collecting stones from such land. He also gives examples of plots of various shapes (Col, V, 1, 13-2, 10) and explains methods of measuring them and planting vines on them. This probably does not refer to centuriated land. Columella may be thinking of the odd corners of a large estate rather than the scraps of marginal land used by *montani* and *rustici*, but the techniques he suggests would have been very useful to them and probably originated among them.

Centuriation in itself may not have restricted or altered significantly the proportion of land in Roman Italy which was used for subsistence farming. Those who received small allocations of centuriated territory were added to the number making a meagre living off the land. Their total was offset by the number of small farmers whose land, taken from them by the Romans, was then allocated in larger portions for commercial ventures. By accepting a small official allotment the peasant farmer may have obtained land of better quality or in a better position than he would otherwise have occupied. In the case of landless citizens from Rome itself, the new allocation may have been infinitely preferable to the *patrimonium* which they or their fathers had left not very long ago, or on which they as younger sons were superfluous. For surely few of the *proletarii* would have attempted to make a living in this way if they or their families had had no previous experi-

ence of country life? The land-hunger of the Roman plebs in the
early Republic can only be explained by the fact that many were
themselves country-bred, or were not many generations removed
from an agricultural or pastoral existence. That cultivable land
of any kind in Italy was becoming scarce by the end of the
Republic and the beginning of the Empire is suggested by the
wistful glances cast upon the broad acres of the barbarians. Horace
writes of the Getae:

> 'immetata quibus iugera liberas
> fruges et Cererem ferunt'.
>
> (*Odes* III, 24, 12-13)

Tacitus (*Germania* XXVI, 1-2) describes the situation among the
Germani: 'They change their plough-lands yearly, and still there
is ground to spare'.[32] Such superfluity of land was characteristic of
the Golden Age (Virgil, *Georgics* I, 125-6):

> 'ne signare quidem aut partiri limite campum
> fas erat'.

The use of the word 'signare' suggests that official surveying of
land was in Virgil's mind when he wrote these lines. The same
idea may underlie Horace's use of 'immetata'. (Ovid, *Metamorphoses* I, 135-6) also represents the official measuring of land as
less desirable than the old, free use of it:

> 'communem prius ceu lumina solis et auras
> cautus humum longo signavit limite mensor'.

Such feelings may sometimes have been aroused by the loss caused
to individuals when land was surveyed and assigned to veterans:

> 'abstulit excultas pertica tristis opes'.
>
> (Propertius, *Elegies* IV, 1, 130)

'Excultas' is an important word in this line: the bitterness is in
the fact that these plots had already been cultivated. Through
the centuries uncultivated patches of land had often changed
hands: this was different. References to land assignment also seem
to have occurred in a wider context. Ofellus (Horace, *Satires* II,
2, 112ff), who took philosophically the position of being a tenant
on the land he had formerly owned, is represented as holding a
radical view of the ownership of land:

> 'nam propriae telluris herum natura illum

nec me nec quemquam statuit'. (120-130)

On the other hand there would seem to have been certain advantages, especially for the smallholder, in occupying centuriated land. The boundaries were carefully laid out and marked. Certain marking-stones might indicate the position of a spring,[33] and a good water supply was more certain to exist near these plots than on the random *agellus*. Irrigation might be facilitated by this, and also by the provision of watercourses and wells. Some compensation was available in the case of flooding and other disasters, by claiming legal redress either from another farmer or from the community. This could not be done in respect of lands which were not part of an official allocation. Some land assignments included rights of pasturage or use of woodland. Burdese in *Studi sull' Ager Publicus* (p. 111) thinks that the sharing of woodland and pasture by a community may be based on a pre-Roman custom. In historical times, however, and particularly when land near to settlements became more scarce, there would be considerable advantage in having such rights recognised and legally enforced.

Notes to Chapter Six

1. Hinrichs concludes (p. 224) that such methods of land division did not originate with the Etruscans or the Romans: they occurred first in the founding of the Latin colonies, an undertaking of the Latin League.
2. R. Martin, *L'Urbanisme dans la Grèce antique*, 2nd ed., 1974, p. 331 (cf. pp. 323-325 on Metapontum). O. A. W. Dilke, *Varro and the Origins of Centuriation*, in *Atti del Congresso internazionale di Studi Varroniani*, Rieti, 1976, p. 357, 'It is now known that the Greek colonies of Sicily and South Italy, such as Metapontum, had a rectangular system of land division both for town and country'.
3. R. Chevallier, *Cité et Territoire*, in *Aufstieg und Niedergang der Römischen Welt*, II, 1, 1974, p. 691. Dilke, *Roman Land Surveyors*, 1971, p. 133, 'It is very probable that centuriation existed in Italy as early as the fourth century BC . . .' cf. *Varro and the Origins of Centuriation*, p. 358, 'It seems possible that first Capua and then the Roman colonies of the late fourth century BC were influenced by the square planning of Hippodamus of Miletus'.
4. Varro, *R.R.* I, 10, 2; Pliny, *N.H.* XVIII, 2 (7).

5. J. Mertens, *Alba Fucens* I, 1969, p. 49; F. Castagnoli, *Orthogonal Town Planning in Antiquity*, 1971, p. 96; *Ippodamo di Mileto*, p. 83; *La Centuriazione di Cosa, Mem. Amer. Acad.* XXIV (1956) p. 163.

6. R. M. Ogilvie, *Early Rome and the Etruscans*, p. 18-19.

7. E. T. Salmon, *Roman Colonization*, p. 42-3.

8. Livy XXXIV, 53, 1, and Strabo VI, 1, 5.

9. The *compascua prossimorum* — see E. Sereni, *Storia del Paesaggio agrario italiano*, p. 27-30.

10. C. Clarke and M. Haswell (*The Economics of Subsistence Agriculture*, p. 54) give 210 kilograms of grain per person per annum as the subsistence minimum.

11. Westrup's theories had been to some extent anticipated by Mommsen, *Römische Geschichte*, I, 1920, p. 183.

12. Trans. J. Falkus, in *Essays in European Economic History* 1500-1800, ed. by Peter Earle, Oxford, 1974.

13. For the existence of such land even in the latter half of the first century BC see C. Hardie, *Roman Florence*, p. 134, in JRS Vol. LV, 1965. This process was legalised for tenants on imperial and private estates by the Mancian Law, introduced probably in the first century AD (Lewis and Reinhold, *Roman Civilization*, Vol. II, p. 179) which may have been an attempt to regulate a common practice.

14. Nenquin, *Salt, A Study in Economic Prehistory*, p. 95.

15. *The Mediterranean*, Vol. I, trans. S. Reynolds, p. 144.

16. As Varro, *R.R.* XVIII, 5, remarks, this example given by Cato is not a standard size of plot. The usual measurement would be 200 *iugera*.

17. He does say (9, 8) that on the suggestion of L. Apustius a third of the land was reserved for later colonists, but this was not necessarily the intention when the land was acquired.

18. 'Quo in genere sicut in ceteris rei publicae partibus est operae pretium diligentiam maiorum recordari, qui colonias sic idoneis in locis contra suspicionem periculi collocarunt, ut esse non oppida Italiae, sed propugnacula imperii viderentur.'

19. In *Res Gestae Divi Augusti* 15, Augustus tells us that he gave 1,000 sesterces to each of his soldiers who were settled in colonies. But these colonists appear to have been already in occupation.

20. *The Roman Land Surveyors*, p. 88-9.

21. F. Castagnoli, *Le 'formae' delle colonie romane e le miniature dei codici dei gromatici, Atti della reale Accademia d'Italia*, series VII, Vol. IV, p. 83-118.

22. *Kerkeosiris: An Egyptian Village in the Ptolemaic Period.*

23. Note here Livy's story of the soldiers who wanted to stay in Campania because the land was of a better quality there (Livy, VII, 38).

24. *Corpus Agrimensorum Romanorum*, ed. C. Thulin (Teubner), pp. 82-3.

25. C. Thulin, op cit., p. 39.

26. cf. 'in relictis possessionibus', Cicero, *De Lege Agraria*, I, 3.

27. Dilke, *The Roman Land Surveyors*, p. 96.

28. The ambiguity surrounding the *loca inculta* is well illustrated by Ovid's use of *incultus* in *Fasti* III, line 192:
'iugeraque inculti pauca tenere soli'.
It means here 'unassigned', 'unoccupied'. The land is going to be cultivated: that is the reason for occupying it.

29. *Maps and Treatises of Roman Land Surveyors, Geographical Journal*, Vol. CXXVII, Part 4, Dec. 1961, p. 420-1.

30. cf. Norman Douglas, *Old Calabria*, p. 156: ' 'La Montagna' is considerably abused all over Italy'.

31. The cultivation of such stony plots seems to have appealed to the imagination of literary men, cf. Strabo, V, 2, 1, who, citing Poseidonius, describes the Ligurians as 'τραχεῖαν γῆν ἀροῦντες, καὶ σκάπτοντες, μᾶλλον δὲ λατομοῦντες.'

32. Penguin Classics translation, by H. Mattingly.

33. Dilke, *The Roman Land Surveyors*, p. 103.

CHAPTER SEVEN

The Baking of Bread

Methods of baking as practised commercially in Roman towns of Italy are well-known and the equipment is familiar from bakeries at Pompeii and Herculaneum. In earlier times, however, baking was done in the home, and it must have continued to be a domestic activity in cottages and small farms at any rate in the remoter areas throughout the Roman period. Pliny (*N.H.* XVIII, 28 (107)) declares that there were no bakers in Rome until the war against Perseus (171-168 BC) and, although we may hesitate to accept a precise date for such a development, he is probably not far from the truth. Whenever the change of usage occurred, it is likely to have been connected with the growth of the urban proletariat and the increased number of families who did not produce their own grain and who lacked suitable cooking facilities. On large landed estates the quantity of bread made to supply the whole work-force would often approximate to that

---

The substance of this chapter has already appeared in 'Antiquity', LII, 1978, under the title 'Home-baking in Roman Italy.'

made by a commercial baker and the same methods would be used. In fact the development of large baking-ovens may well have begun on the estates before such apparatus was in common use in towns. The self-sufficiency which was the aim of the landed proprietor (Varro, *R.R.* I, 22) led to the practice and development of various trades in a 'sheltered' situation, and baking was one of them.

How then did the Italian peasants living outside the towns between the sixth century BC and the second century AD bake their bread? At the beginning of this period Iron Age conditions prevail and dwellings are such as the hut-urns portray, or the Iron Age huts on the Palatine (Gjerstad, *Early Rome* III, p. 33ff). In the recent excavations at Narce part of a domed clay oven was found (*A Faliscan Town in South Etruria*, T. W. Potter, pp. 68 and 104) which is thought to have been used for domestic purposes. It is provisionally dated c. 600 BC. Many Iron Age huts have a central hearth, though in some it is on one side of the building, and it is at floor-level or below. There was no very effective outlet for the smoke, though some of the hut-urns show holes for this purpose. There probably remained at the beginning of the Roman period some of the terracotta cooking stands of the type recently found at Acquarossa and other sites in the neighbourhood of Viterbo. These were usually semi-cylindrical, with projecting supports to hold a cooking-vessel. The stands were placed in the embers of a wood or charcoal fire on an open hearth (C. Scheffer, *Cooking Stands and some possibly related objects from Acquarossa, Opuscula Romana*, XI, 1976, p. 39-52). Some hearths of the Roman period were at floor level or only slightly above it, including that in the kitchen of the *villa rustica* at Boscoreale (Mau-Kelsey, *Pompeii*, pp. 355-6) which is in the centre of the room. In general, however, the type of hearth seems to have changed with the style of the building. Smoke continued to be troublesome in rural dwellings in the classical period: Horace, *Satires* I, 5, 80-1, describes a stove 'lacrimoso non sine fumo'. 'Stove' in this passage is *caminus*, a word taken directly from Greek and applicable to anything from a smelting furnace to a baking-oven. Here it probably refers to the raised hearth on which a fire of wood or charcoal burned. Beneath it was space for keeping a supply of fuel. (A. Maiuri, *Ercolano, I Nuovi Scavi* (1927-58), p. 311, fig. 244, and p. 340, fig. 269). *Caminus* could also in some contexts indicate a closed-flame stove with one aperture on the top for the pan, and one at the side for stoking the fire. This must have developed from the raised hearth, but is quite different from it. This type of closed-flame stove could not have been used for baking and would have been supplemented by a *furnus* or used in a town house where bread was obtained from a commercial bakery. The difficulty of the smoke-filled room was an old one, hence the 'blackened beams' of which the poets were fond (Virgil, *Ecl.* VII, 49-50; Ovid, *Fasti* V, 505) and the hams and sausages being smoked in the *carnarium* which hung from the rafters (Cato, *De Agri Cultura*, 162, 3; Varro, *Res Rusticae*, I, 45; *App. Verg. Moretum*, 55).

The fire was banked up to last when the family went out or retired for the night ('contectus ignis', Pliny, *N.H.* XVIII, 84 (358) cf. Lucretius, IV, 926-8). It was kept burning continually, like its national symbol, the fire in the temple of Vesta at Rome. The Vestal Virgins who tended this were the counterpart of the women and girls throughout Italy who were responsible for keeping the fire going at home. If the fire went out, it was usual to rekindle it by borrowing from a neighbour — hence the determination of the miser in Plautus' *Aulularia*, 91-2, to have his fire extinguished so that no one could borrow it. Plautus alludes to this practice also in the *Trinummus*, 3, 2, 53: 'Fire is given to you, even if you seek it from a personal enemy'. In the poets fire is often being aroused from yesterday's ashes (Virgil, *Aeneid* V, 745; Ovid, *Met.* VIII, 642; App. Verg. *Moretum*, 8-12). It was important to keep the fire going as it was difficult to relight it. Matches were available in Rome in the Imperial period, but earlier and in remote places flint and tinder were the main resource (Virgil, *Aen.* I, 176; Lucretius, VIII, 776; Pliny, *N.H.* XVI, 40, 77 (208)). The grammarians when discussing the meaning of *focus* (hearth) are emphatic about this task of 'looking after' the fire. Servius (commenting on Virgil, *Aen.* III, 134) says *focus* is derived from *fotu*, because the fire is 'looked after' there. Isidore (*Diff. Verb.*

307) says the same, and attributes this strange piece of etymology to Varro. In *De Vita Populi Romani* I (p. 252, 196, *Grammaticae Romanae Fragmenta,* ed. Funaioli) we read: 'The kitchen was at the back of the house, and takes its name from the fact that the fire was looked after there'.

On the low hearth must originally have developed the method of baking bread on leaves or pieces of tile: at any rate it would be less easy to heap up the fire on the raised hearth to cover the food. It would be easier to maintain a steady warmth for this purpose in a cooking-pit than on a raised platform. Ovid in *Fasti* VI, 315-6 refers to this type of baking as being at ground-level: 'The bread, placed beneath the ashes was baked by the hearth itself: broken pieces of tile had been spread on the warm ground'. (cf. *Apicius, L'Art culinaire,* Jacques André, para. 397). 'The hearth itself' is emphasised in contrast to other methods of baking bread which involved the use of the *testu* or an oven. Leaves on which bread was baked would have to be of a wholesome variety, and Columella in some of his recipes suggests bay-leaves. This may have led to the practice of using different types of leaf, to vary the flavour of the loaf. This is certainly stated by Pliny (XX, 72 (185)) with reference to anise, and in XIX, 53 (168) he writes of a method of baking in which poppy seed is placed on top of the loaf, and celery and coriander underneath it. This seems over-elaborate, especially as it is said to produce 'country bread'. The second passage is somewhat obscure, because unlike the other statements as to what was put under loaves, this one could refer to seeds rather than leaves. Yet although coriander seed was used in baking, it is more likely to have been the leaves of celery which were meant. Pliny may have confused two processes here. Baking on leaves must have been common practice for a long period, since Cato, Pliny, Columella and Apicius all mention it as a normal procedure. Cato (LXXVI) in a recipe for cheese pastry suggests oiling the leaves. This would not have been desirable if the baking was to be done on the open hearth, but in this case a cover is to be used.

Baking in the ashes is well described by William Cobbett,

writing at the beginning of the nineteenth century (in *Cottage Economy*, p. 204 of the 1926 edition):

'These are baked as follows: open a place in the side of a wood fire on the hearth, and having put in the cakes, each between two cabbage leaves, lay them on the hot hearth, sprinkle some ashes lightly over first, then put hot coals on the top, and if these appear to cool fast, remove them from time to time, and replace them with hotter coals from the fire . . . I have been told that in Devonshire and in some other parts of the country, it is or was the custom, in cottages and farm houses, to bake bread on the hearth, large loaves as well as cakes, covering the loaf close with an iron, or brown earthenware vessel'.

The method with which Cobbett ends his description involves the use of a vessel known to the Romans as a *testu* or *testum*. This was an earthenware crock which was placed over the food to be baked, in the manner of the 'chicken-brick' sometimes used nowadays. The *testu* stood in the hot ashes of the fire. We are not told whether it was a vessel made for the purpose, or whether any strong pot could be used if it was large enough. This method was employed for cooking vegetables and meat as well as baking. Cato, in *De Agri Cultura*, Chapter 74, suggests the use of the *testu* for baking bread, and in Chapter 75 for a cake. Here the cake is to be placed on leaves and then put under a crock. In short the *testu* is a refinement on the simple baking in the ashes. Ovid (*Fasti* V, 461) has vegetables cooking under it, and as they are 'foaming' it would appear that they are being boiled or braised rather than baked. The *testu* seems both in name and nature to have arisen from the use of tiles or potsherds either below or above the food to be baked. In the Virgilian poem *Moretum* the tiles are placed over the food (line 51) and the fire is heaped on top of them.

An interesting development arising from this is the small oven forming part of the kitchen stove, as in the *Casa dei due atri* at Herculaneum. This stove is described in detail by Maiuri (*I Nuovi Scavi*, p. 277, and fig. 221). Maiuri does not think this oven was used for bread but for meat and cakes. It appears to be as it were a stationary model of the *testu* and a stage on the way to the development of the larger ovens.

The *testu*, as we can see from the Roman agricultural writers, continued to be used after other methods of baking had become common. These included the *furnus* and the *clibanus*. There was also the *fornax*, and mention of this brings us to another important point in the history of baking. The *fornax* was the large oven used for baking the grain after it had been harvested, to improve its keeping qualities and to dry it so that it was easier to grind. Ovid, *Fasti* II, 389ff, describes what happened before ovens were used for this purpose, when, as he supposes, the grain was parched on the open hearth. Ashes were gathered up in mistake for grain, and sometimes the houses themselves caught fire. The *fornax* must have been a great improvement upon such methods, and it is not surprising that a festival, the *Fornacalia*, should have arisen to celebrate it. These ovens would be shared among groups of farms or a village, and therefore a communal festival could be held in connection with them. The *Fornacalia* was associated with the Sabines and Pliny (XVIII, 2 (7)) says that it was established by Numa. This may simply be another way of saying that its origin is uncertain but that it did not come from Etruria or Magna Graecia. It certainly implies that the use of grain-drying ovens was of considerable antiquity in Central Italy. The earliest *pistores*, as in Plautus, were millers, and must have used these ovens. When they became bakers in the towns they used a *furnus* which had much in common with the drying-oven. They adopted the same sort of wooden instrument for inserting the bread into the oven as they had used before to stir the grain in the storeroom. The baker's oven was in fact very similar to the pizza oven of Campania at the present day. Town-dwellers in ancient Italy, like their modern counterparts, may have taken their own food to the baker to be cooked. A passage of Horace (*Satires* I, 4, lines 37-40) may imply this, but if it was a common practice, it is surprising that it did not attract the attention of the satirists more often: instead they concentrate on the shops selling ready-cooked food. If the bakehouse was used for cooking the family meal, it would help to explain the lack of cooking facilities in the *insulae*.

The household oven originally formed part of the *focus*, but there would not have been room for it on the *focus brevis* to which Juvenal alludes (XI, 79). In the rural setting the family hearth was supplemented by fires made outdoors or in an outbuilding, especially at the time of the vintage and the olive harvest. Cato, in giving instructions for the making of a pesticide specifically states that it should be heated out-of-doors, because the mixture may flare up. In villas and on the larger farms a *furnus* similar to the baker's oven was used and it was separate from the *focus*. The portable ovens found at Pompeii, and mentioned by Petronius, were the equipment of wealthy households, not of the ordinary family. They may have developed from the portable hearth or brazier which both literary and archaeological sources associate with the Etruscans, and which was in use from the sixth century onwards. The portable oven as known to the Romans later was the *clibanus*, which is by its very name Greek. André (op. cit., note to para. 272, p. 191) describes the *clibanus* in terms reminiscent of the *testu*. However, Apicius distinguishes three types of oven, the *furnus*, the *clibanus* and the *thermospodium*, and recommends the use of each of them as occasion demands. The *thermospodium* seems to have been a more sophisticated name for the *testu* or for a similar contrivance. As the *thermospodium* is usually said by Apicius to be 'above and below' the food, it must have had a lower portion on which the food was placed. We know from Columella (V, 10, 4) that the *clibanus* was wider at the bottom than at the top, and from Herodotus (II, 92) that it could become red-hot.

On small-holdings and in cottages then, during the Roman period, bread was baked in the ashes, or under a crock, or in more prosperous farmsteads, in an oven either separate from or part of a *focus*. As to the nature of the bread itself, its main constituent, grain, has been the subject of detailed discussion elsewhere. N. Jasny, however (in *The Daily Bread of the Ancient Greeks and Romans*, Osiris, IX (1950) p. 231) thinks that there has been a general tendency to overestimate the importance of wheat in classical antiquity as compared with other grains. He points out that even in modern times only a minority can afford to use the kind of grain they prefer. The rest use that which can be produced locally with the least labour or on the smallest area of land. Though much has been written about the grain content of the loaf, less attention has been directed to its other ingredients, salt and leaven.

Salt was not always an ingredient of Italian bread in Roman times. It is used by the countryman in the *Moretum,* but it does not appear in the recipe for 'kneaded bread' in Cato. The fact that salt was often eaten as a relish with bread may suggest that the bread itself did not necessarily contain salt. Although no part of Italy is very far from the coast, it must have been quite difficult to maintain a continuous supply of salt in remote places. Distribution depended on pedlars following age-old tracks from the salt-pans to the interior of the country, or in northern Italy from the salt-mines of central Europe, and they would have to be paid. Hence the importance of the *salarium,* for salt was one of the commodities for which ready cash, or some widely-accepted medium of exchange, was needed. It could not be paid for in kind, as the miller was paid by a portion of the grain, and the buying of salt would therefore have been one of the few cash transactions essential to the livelihood of the peasant farmer. When it was not available he used wood-ash, as Pliny and others tell us. The salt-box was as important in the Roman household as the tea-caddy used to be in England. Horace (*Odes,* II, 16, lines 11-12) thinks of it as being handed down from father to son. It is also regarded by Persius (*Satires* III, 25) as part of a man's inheritance. But the salt was transported in some other container. Frontinus (*Strategemata,* III, 14, 3) has an interesting anecdote about jars of salt being floated along the river at the siege of Mutina. It is possible, however, that this salt was for preserving meat, since animals were also floated down the river to provide food in that emergency.

A variety of raising-agents were used by the Romans in making bread. There was also some unleavened bread, made of coarsely-ground flour. This was considered more nourishing and had longer keeping qualities, which would have been important for shepherds who had to carry a supply of food with them. Pliny mentions some bread produced in the neighbourhood of Ancona, which was made of groats, steeped, kneaded with raisin juice and then baked in pots which were afterwards broken in order to extract it. This bread was soaked before use, like the hard bread used in sheep-rearing districts in Greece, Crete, S. Italy and Sardinia today. The breaking of the pot, which is not uncommon in ancient recipes, could be an expedient required where oil was not easily available. Cato already knew of the practice of greasing the dish (LXXXIV), but it is of course only appropriate to the use of an open dish, as in this example, or a very wide-necked jar. The only feature of Roman bread which Athenaeus (*Deipnosophistae*, III, 108ff) mentions in his monumental list of types of bread is that it was 'quartered' before it was baked. This is the kind of loaf found in Pompeii, divided into segments, originally for easy distribution among the family at an informal meal. It was no doubt an improvement on earlier less shapely loaves, probably large and dirty like those which Athenaeus attributes to the Cilicians. The indentations could be made with the fingers, as Athenaeus (*Deipnosophistae*, III, 108c) says that lines were made on certain rolls, or with a reed, which Columella recommends for slicing fruit and vegetables, and Apicius for cutting up *foie gras*.

According to Pliny (XVIII, 26 (102)) the raising-agent used by most households in his own time was a portion of the dough kept from the previous day's baking. This would ferment in hot weather, but it would have to be kept moist. Such dough would already itself have been leavened. A special raising-agent could be made by boiling flour and water (without salt) and leaving it to go sour. Pliny also gives more complicated methods of making leaven, one from millet, and the other from a barley-cake kept in a pot until it is sour and then soaked in water. Athenaeus (III, 113c) allows time in one recipe for the dough to rise before it is put in the oven. As this bread is mushroom-shaped it has probably risen more than was usual.

Bread, and some kinds of pastry or scone dough, were kneaded, and this in some recipes, as in the *panis depsticius* of Cato, takes the place of leaven. The function of the kneading is to let air into the mixture. The Latin word for this process is *depsere*, derived from Greek. It is onomatopoeic, and represents the sound made when the dough is turned over and slapped down on the surface upon which it is being kneaded. The turning-over is specifically mentioned when the word *transversare* is used, as in the *Moretum* line 46. The use of this word in reference to cookery is similar to the use of *versare* and *conversare* in Apicius. The former describes the turning of a chicken onto a dish, the latter the 'turning out' of a savoury mousse from a mould. *Depsere* and *condepsere* have ante-classical usages, as one would expect for such a basic process, but why are they Greek derivatives? Probably because in earlier Italian homes a porridge rather than bread was made from the grain. The word does however suggest some contact with the Greek language at a very early stage, either by way of Etruria or Magna Graecia. The later Roman words for kneading are all adapted for this use while having many other commoner meanings. They appear in some cases to be makeshifts employed by literary men who had only a superficial understanding of the process. *Subigere* is one of these. Pliny in XVIII, 27 (105) uses it to mean 'soften', when adding eggs and milk to special kinds of bread-dough. This may be parallel to its use for softening hides, but neither the purpose nor the method of these activities is the same as that of kneading dough. *Tractare* or *trahere* would appear to have had a more technical use in connection with baking since *tracta* is the name of a kind of cake. This process took the place of our 'rolling out', and *trahere* describes the intention of this accurately. It is however more appropriate to pastry-making than to the baking of bread.

These are some of the considerations which arise from a study of home-baking in Roman times. Its development in general is summed up by Seneca (*Epist. Mor.* XC, 23) when he describes in the words of Posidonius how grain was first milled. He ends with this account of man's invention of the baking-oven; 'and he made bread, which was at first baked in the warm ashes or on a red-hot tile, then ovens were gradually invented and other apparatus which depends on heat for its use'. The word 'gradually' here reminds us what a good understanding the ancients themselves had of the painstaking process of early invention. More will be learned about types of hearth and stove as excavation in town and country in Italy proceeds. For methods of cooking we are mainly dependent upon literary evidence. No apology is needed for using the testimony of the poets on this subject. As Pierre Grimal has said (*A la recherche de l'Italie antique,* Paris 1961) their descriptions of ancient dwellings received remarkable corroboration from the discoveries on the Palatine, and were probably based on observation of extant examples as well as on oral and written tradition. Their references to contemporary arrangements are likely to be at least equally sound. It is often supposed that we have very little information about cookery and household matters in the Roman period. Yet there are few other practical subjects upon which we have written accounts extending from the second century BC to the early Empire, as well as an ever increasing quantity of archaeological material.

CHAPTER EIGHT

Houses and Outbuildings on the Small Farm

In considering farmhouses and farm-buildings we shall be chiefly concerned with those in use on small farms or inhabited by peasants living at subsistence level. The fully-developed villa with the *atrium* is well-known, both from the pages of Vitruvius and from modern expositions.[1] Such villas were not the dwellings of the poor either in the suburban areas or in the country, and although they vary considerably in size and elaboration they do not constitute examples of the kind of farm we are discussing. The *villa rustica* of the type recently excavated in Campania is more relevant to the life of the peasant farmer, but most of these were probably owned by absentee proprietors and managed by a *vilicus*. Their possible evolution from a simpler building, mentioned by White (*Roman Farming* pp. 418 and 424) is interesting (cf. McKay, op. cit., pp. 17-22). We do not receive much information on this subject from the agronomists as they, with the possible exception of Cato, are concerned with the larger establishments and with profitable business enterprises. Cato (XIV and XV) gives advice to the owner who wishes to build a new

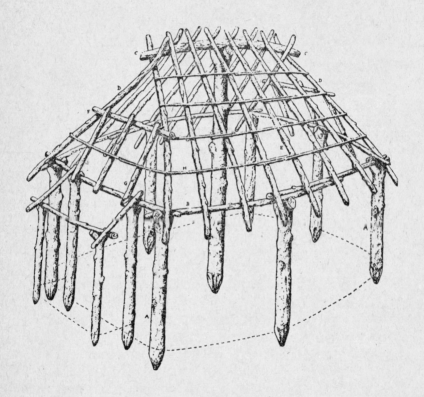

6. Reconstruction of the framework of an Iron Age hut found on the Germalus, Rome (*Monumenti antichi*, XL1, 1951) Note the *columen* (c) and the projecting porch.

steading, but it is on a fairly ambitious scale, and the assumption is made that the farmer will be employing a contractor to do the work. The only reminder of a more primitive system is the arrangement that the farmer is to supply all the materials and the saw and plumb line. It is a prosperous farmstead, for the house is to have windows with shutters, there are to be cattle stalls, a stable and accommodation for slaves. He mentions the possibility of building the upper part of the wall from one foot above ground in brick. This does not necessarily imply luxury or extravagance: these bricks would in many areas be made on the premises, by the method which Palladius describes in VI, 12, and dried in the sun. The instructions which Cato gives in CXXVIII for plastering a 'habitatio' probably refer to a building of this kind. Varro (I, 13, 6-7) considers the methods of building villas in his time extravagant, or at least he put this opinion into the mouth of Fundanius. He is not criticising the mode of construction of the materials used but the arrangement of rooms and the accommodation provided. In the past, he says, the important parts of the farmstead were the kitchen, stables and cellars for wine and oil: now they are luxurious dining-rooms.

To discover the type of rural dwelling used by many of the Italians at any rate at the beginning of the Roman period we have to go back to the Iron Age huts, such as those found on the Palatine, which date from the earliest years of the united city.[2] For even within the city boundaries at that time there was a rural way of life. These huts are not merely an interesting curiosity, but an indication of the kind of building which must have existed in the countryside long after more sophisticated methods had been adopted in the towns. The *casa Romuli* on the Palatine[3] was not exhibited for the admiration of later Romans because they could not in their own day see a thatched hut in use, but because such a great man as Romulus had lived in one. Our literary sources do not describe the construction of such huts, probably because they were quite commonplace at the time, but the details are available to us now from the excavated examples. The floor of the hut was rectangular and below ground-level, dug out from the solid rock. The post holes indicate that two uprights, standing within the space excavated from the rock, supported a *columen* (ridge-pole) from which the roof sloped down on either side to meet a low wattle or stone wall. The *columen* was shorter than the total length of the building, as there was an extension with a doorway at the front of the hut. The roof timbers would be covered with thatch consisting of reeds or brushwood. This accords with our literary references as well as bearing certain resemblances to types of rural buildings existing in Italy in recent times. It is also imitated in the *Tomba della Capanna* at Cerveteri (end of the seventh century BC) where the *columen* can be clearly seen. The tomb has 'benches' of pebbles on either side of it, which probably represented the sleeping-places in the huts, on which straw, reeds, branches or skins might be spread.[4] Other examples of this kind have been found by excavation, as well as a modern instance in shepherds' huts in Sicily.[5]

Constructions of a somewhat similar type have been found by Ostenberg at Luni sul Mignone, near Viterbo. He describes two of these, which belong to the Iron Age. Hut I, on the site called Tre Erici[6] was rectangular and rather like the Palatine huts. Hut II was oval and the holes for the wattle framework of its walls have been found. The dating of Hut II (carbon 14) places it at the end of the eighth century BC or the beginning of the seventh. Other huts were found on the acropolis of the town and these date from Apennine I to the Iron Age. These huts all have their bases excavated from the solid rock. Ostenberg thinks that this may have been carried out by communal effort since the inhabitants were living in clans. The most unusual feature of these huts is the rock-floor and its level, and it is interesting to note that Palladius, writing a thousand years later, describes the same method of building (VIII, De Aedificio). He is explaining how to build a work-room on the farm, referring to it as a *fabrica* and also as a *praetorium*. It can be built, he says, on foundations cut out of rock, and they are to be one or two feet in depth. Palladius suggests that this can be done 'si lapis vel tofus occurrat'. This building is for temporary occupation only. Some sort of covering must have been laid over the foundation rock, because (IX) it is to have a floor on which the slaves can work with bare feet even in winter. Another type of rural dwelling has been found at Acquarossa, six kilometres north of Viterbo.[7] The settlement is dated to the second half of the seventh century BC and was destroyed and abandoned before 500 BC. Hut A (in Zone B) measures approximately 12 × 10 m and contains three rooms in a row, with a narrow vestibule in front of them. The largest was the kitchen, with the hearth in a corner, and probably a chimney built into the wall. The foundations of the huts are usually of tufo blocks, but some are excavated from the rock. The walls are of stone, tufo, sun-dried brick, pisé or wattle-and-daub, depending no doubt on what was available and what could be afforded. The roofs were of tiles on a wooden framework. There were two main types of hearth, one recessed into the wall, the other central, with a smoke-hole in the roof which had a movable cover.

Another kind of archaeological evidence for the early types of rural dwelling is provided by the hut-urns found on many sites in Etruria and Latium. These represent buildings roughly contemporary with those discussed above, belong to the same areas and have much in common with them. They are a simplification and do not necessarily give us the plan of a complete dwelling, or the relation of one house to another in a village. However the urns show very clearly the arrangement of the wooden roof-rafters, and the general shape of the huts. An example from Grottaferrata, from the Villa Cavaletti in the Alban Hills (P. G. Gierow, *The Iron Age Culture of Latium*, II, p. 53) has an almost circular ground-plan and a convex top ridge on the roof. Three ridge logs on either side of this meet in pairs above it. Angular ribs representing logs were used to weigh down the thatched roof (pp. 52-4). As in all the hut-urns from this area, the door was closed by a rectangular slab, attached to the door-posts by a cord or pin passed through holes in projections from those posts. The hut-urns from Grottaferrata and the neighbourhood belong to the sixth and seventh centuries BC.

The wicker-work walls of any of the types of dwelling we have mentioned were coated with clay to make them more waterproof (as in Petronius, *Satyricon*, 135).[8] Some idea of the flimsiness of this type of building is conveyed by Plautus, *Mostellaria*, 101-149.

Philolaches, somewhat the worse for his riotous living, is comparing a man to a house. This is not necessarily a rural dwelling, but the comparison, depending upon the way in which damp permeates the walls of a house until they collapse, must represent a matter of common experience, or the point of the joke would be lost. This is a building with a tiled roof, and another such, called a villa, is described by Plautus in the *Rudens*, lines 83-123. The house has been destroyed by a storm, and is to be mended with clay dug up on the spot:

'luto usust multo, multam terram confode'.   (line 100)

Although the roof was tiled, it is suggested that it could be covered with reeds cut in the local marsh:

'quin tu in paludem is exicasque harundinem
qui pertegamus villam, dum sudumst'.   (lines 122-3)

There seem to be some reminiscences of the older type of rural building in literature. The Younger Pliny (*Epist.* VIII, 17) writing of an occasion when the Tiber was in flood, says that there were 'villarum trabes atque culmina varie lateque fluitantia'. Are these *culmina,* which float, the thatched coverings of the smaller houses and cottages? Or are they the roof-beams of a classical villa from which the tiles have fallen away? Seneca (*Epist. Mor.* XC, 10) knew exactly how the ancient dwellings were built: 'Furcae utrimque suspensae fulciebant casam'. The cottage in Ovid, *Fasti* IV, 627ff, is called a villa, and yet it is described as 'stantem tibicine', surely a reference to a light wooden framework, or to a covering of reeds? In Latin poetry the word *subire* is often user of entering a poor dwelling, and much emphasis is placed on its being *humilis*. In English the idea of a poor dwelling being 'low' as well as 'lowly' arises because the houses of the wealthy had several storeys, and were often reached by a flight of steps. The houses of wealthy Romans, however, were of one or two storeys and their height was not an important feature. Was the poorer rural dwelling still built with its floor below ground-level in classical times, or was this a linguistic relic of the pre-historic custom? There seems to be no doubt in the minds of the poets that cottages in the country were thatched.[9] In the Virgilian *Priapea* III, 1-2, the *villula* is thatched with withes and reeds, although the shepherd's hut in Virgil, *Eclogues* I, 68, is roofed with turves. Methods would vary in different localities, use being made of the materials most easily available. The custom of using roof-space as a convenient storage area and of hanging household equipment from the rafters must have arisen when the roughly-trimmed boughs formed an intricate framework for the thatched *culmen*. There would have been plenty of handy projections as well as the solid ridge-pole and its uprights. In Horace, *Satires* II, 2, 122, raisins are described by the use of the adjective *pensilis* because they were dried by hanging them in the rafters.[10] The home of Baucis and Philemon was supposedly in Phrygia, but Ovid's description of it (*Met.* VIII, 629-659) probably owes much to the cottages he knew in Italy. It was thatched with straw and reeds (line 130). Dry branches for the fire were brought down from the roof — Ovid does not say whether they were stored outside or inside it. The old man then reaches down the bacon from the rafters with a forked stick. In Virgil, *Georgics* II, the baskets for soil-testing are to be taken down from the smoky roof-space (l. 242, 'fumosis deripe tectis'). In *Georgics* I, lines 174-5, the plough handle is hung over the hearth to be seasoned.

Allied to this is the use of the rafters for storage on the *carnarium*, a device which continued to be used throughout the Roman period.[11] The *carnarium* consisted of one or more long pieces of wood suspended from the roof, usually over the hearth, from which meat was hung until required for cooking. Bacon and sausages might be smoked in this way. In Juvenal XI, 82, the pork is 'rara pendentia crate', the *carnarium* being here a wicker rack hanging from the ceiling. Apicius does not use the term *carnarium* in his recipes, but suggests hanging sausages *ad fumum*, and this was probably done in the kitchen or storeroom and not in the living-space of the house. The custom has been maintained, for in the spring of 1975 in the kitchen of a small trattoria at Lanuvio a *carnarium*, consisting of a roughly-trimmed branch suspended by wires from the ceiling in front of the stove, was to be seen. A string of sausages was looped over it.

That an early type of rural dwelling, either rounded or rectangular, with thatched roof and wicker or stone walls, persisted seems likely not only from literary references, but from the existence of such buildings in recent times in Italy.[12] Thomas Ashby, who was one of the first to note the similarities, wrote of the 'thatched conical huts in which shepherds from the Abruzzi live' (*The Roman Campagna in Classical Times*, p. 51) and (pp. 135-6) 'The huts . . . which are inhabited by peasant labourers from the hills, may give an image of those in which the primitive population must have dwelt'. Some of these simple structures exist today but are used to contain hay or farm implements rather than as dwelling-houses. If they are used for human habitation, it is generally of a temporary nature. In *La Casa rurale nell' Umbria*, p. 77, F. Bonasera describes in detail two huts (which are illustrated in the same volume on p. 76, fig. 17). On p. 131 under the heading 'Dimore temporanee' he writes of the huts which the shepherds build for their temporary accommodation in the hills. These are rectangular stone buildings with a gabled roof, and two or three rooms. These huts serve the same purpose as the Scottish 'bothy'.

Much more like the ancient dwellings to which we have referred are those discussed by A. Cervesato (*Latina Tellus: La Campagna Romana*, p. 176). They are also illustrated. There is an oblong hut with a ridge-pole and frame in the ancient manner. On subsequent pages whole villages of these huts are shown. Cervesato also mentions harvesters' huts. As for the ancient method of cutting foundations or floors from rock, M. Prete and M. Fondi (*La Casa rurale nel Lazio settentrionale e nell'agro romano*) write of dwellings cut out of the 'tufi' at Celleno and Lubriano, which at the time of writing (1957) were mostly deserted or only temporarily inhabited. However these are more in the nature of cave dwellings than huts on stone foundations.

Quite a different type of small farmhouse was the tall, narrow building shown in stucco decorations, such as those from the Casa Farnesina in Rome,[13] and in wall paintings from Rome and Campania. Some have supposed that all these buildings were part of the fanciful landscapes, often of Egyptian inspiration, which were popular in villa decoration in the early Empire, but there is some reason for thinking that in certain examples they represent a type of farmhouse which existed at any rate in South Italy. M. Borda (*La Pittura romana,* p. 207) thinks that the paintings show Egyptian influence, but that they are not set in Egypt because of the hills and small streams shown in them, with fishermen drawing in their nets. He regards them as fanciful Hellenistic scenes. He also thinks that Roman painters (such as the artist mentioned by Pliny, *N.H.* XXXV, 37 (116)) may have changed these scenes from an ideal to a real countryside. One of the more realistic examples is shown in *Römische Wandmalerei* by F. Wirth, p. 148, plate 76. This is dated 200-220 AD. Some are earlier than this, and in general this house-style seems to belong to the early Empire and was probably found mainly in South Italy and on the coastal plain of the Tyrrhenian Sea. It may have been introduced through Hellenistic influence originating in Egypt, but could also have been a response to the marshy and malarial conditions of the coastlands of Western Italy at that time.[14] The houses are stone-built with flat roofs, narrow, with apparently a room or rooms on the first floor for the human inhabitants, and a space for animals or storage on the ground floor, which has a fairly large, central door. The existence of such buildings becomes more probable in view of the excavated farm sites which we shall discuss later.

A particularly interesting representation of a group of farm buildings is discussed by W. J. T. Peters in *Landscape in Romano-Campanian Mural Painting.* This is the first *intercolumnium* next to the rear wall of the Sala del Monochromo in the House of Livia at Rome. Of it Peters (op. cit., p. 41, referring to fig. 30) writes: 'Further to the right we see a group of houses in the background with only here and there a door or a window. This part might have been painted in Italy in the present time as far as the subject is concerned . . . Yet it is certainly not based entirely on phantasy'. It should be noted that the lack of doors and windows in one of these buildings arises from the fact that we are viewing it from the rear. The entrance was presumably on the other side. The date of these buildings is thought to lie between 30 and 25 BC.[15]

If we turn now to the archaeological evidence for the small stone-built rural dwelling, we shall find that in recent years greater attention has been paid to the recording and excavation of this type of building in Italy. Discussion at this point is necessarily incomplete, but certain very interesting facts are already coming to light. In *Capena and the Ager Capenas*[16] G. D. B. Jones describes a Roman building of limestone and mortar, with a single main room (6.70 × 6.35 m) still standing, and a small extension on the N.W. side. He writes: 'The structure represents a small farm building of the early first century AD and corresponds in general with the ground-plan of the peasants' farmhouses occasionally seen in Pompeian wall paintings, e.g. the tower-shaped rustic house depicted in the *Casa della Fontana piccola*'. He considers that the modern farms of the Ente Maremma and the Cassa per il Mezzogiorno are still clearly related to this tradition.

In the second part of this article[17] Jones describes the excavation of a typical small farm. Five sites were examined on the Monte Forco ridge, and, as none was appreciably larger than the rest, as a preliminary judgement he considers it unlikely that one farm belonged to a landlord and the others to his tenants. To show the size of these farms he has marked the area of a *iugerum* on the plan (reproduced on page 126). The holdings in question appear to have been not much larger than 5-6 *iugera*. The detailed description of one of the farms is as follows. The dwelling house was probably of a single storey, with the roof more likely to have been pitched than flat. 'A farmer at the lower end of the agricultural scale with which we are dealing was unlikely to have owned much livestock, but the doorway is wide enough (2.60 m) to have accommodated an ox, if animals lived alongside humans in the interior.' (Jones, op. cit., p. 157). Post holes outside this building probably indicate the postition of a lean-to on the E side where agricultural implements or livestock were kept. The farm dates from the early part of the Augustan period and continued to be occupied in the late first century AD.

The smaller of the two villas excavated at Francolise in 1962-4 appears to have been similar to this, particularly in having a farmyard attached to it. (PBSR, XX, 1965, p. 55-69, van Blanckenhagen, Cotton and Ward Perkins). The first phase of the Posto villa is described as follows (p. 67): '. . . a simple farmhouse, with the living quarters occupying one wing and lean-to sheds or porticoes, for the storage of crops, carts and farm implements or for the stalling of farm animals, grouped around the other three sides of a central courtyard. The more substantially built rooms at the south-east corner could have served as extra living-quarters for the farm-labourers. On the basis of the associated pottery the first occupation of the Posto site may be dated to the period between 120 and 80 BC.' This is clearly a larger establishment than those which we have previously mentioned, but it is included here for comparison, offering as it does another example of a farmyard surrounded by outbuildings.[18] In course of time no doubt further rural dwellings will be excavated and examined and, if our impression that styles vary in different localities is correct, there may well be other designs to add to the selection given here.

The general conclusion must be that the earliest rural dwellings in Roman Italy were of wood, with a thatched roof and wattle or stone walls. Where it existed rock was utilised for foundations. At all times the style of building varied according to the locality and the materials available. By the end of the Republic most farms were stone-built, with outbuildings of similar construction. Temporary buildings, shepherds' huts and the homes of the *montani* would continue to be constructed in the primitive manner. Greek influence in South Italy produced more elaborate stone buildings and was probably responsible for the tower-like structures, in which, as in medieval and modern times, the lower storey was used for stabling and storage. The small farms which have been mapped and in some cases excavated, have up to the present time usually been located on or near Roman roads. This has arisen naturally since the roads themselves were being traced and studied. There were, however, many other cottages and farm plots, some widely scattered, and, as nowadays, not served by any paved road. An example of this can be seen on the map of Sutri and its neighbourhood provided by G. Duncan to illustrate his article on this area. (*Sutri (Sutrium)*, PBSR, XIII, 1958, p. 78.

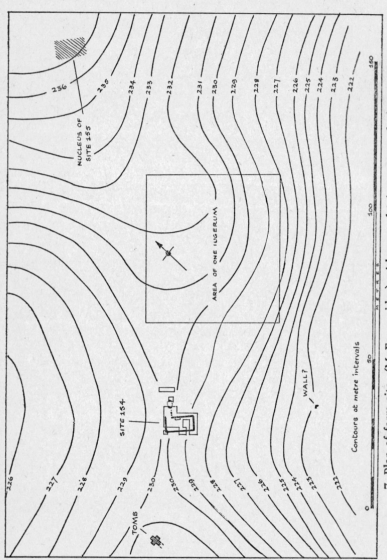

7. Plan of farm sites (M. Forco ridge) with area of 1 *iugerum* marked on it.
from: *Capena and the Ager Capenas*, Part II, by G. D. B. Jones, in PBSR Vol. XVIII (1963). p. 148.

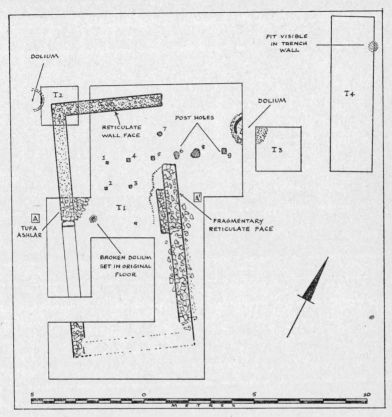

8. (M. Forco: Excavation Plan of Site 154)

cf. K. D. White, *Roman Farming*, p. 386, where a map is reproduced showing the north-eastern Ager Veientanus and the contrast
between the villa sites along roads and the smaller farms mostly
at a distance from them.) Particularly interesting is the continuity
of use of these sites, and even of the buildings themselves. At map
reference 688850 (Duncan, p. 101) the Roman brick walls on
rough concrete foundations 'have been re-used as the basis of a
modern straw hut'. Again at 701855 (p. 107) 'Three walls of a
rectangular concrete building survive, incorporated in the foundations of a modern barn'. At 716870 (p. 113) a Roman cistern was
found. 'At present it serves as a hut, and has had a straw roof

added to it.' The large number of Roman cisterns or parts of them which have been observed, as well as the *cuniculi* which were common in this part of Etruria, show the importance of water-storage and irrigation on all these farms, whatever their size or type.

At present only a few areas have been studied in this way, and most of these are in Etruria. Such studies are based upon surface indications only and other buildings are likely to have existed of which no traces are now visible, because they are concealed by woodland or later habitations. Added to the other evidence we have mentioned they help to give some impression, however incomplete, of the nature of the premises occupied by the small-holder. It is important for the understanding of the whole of the Roman period in Italy to remember the existence of such farm-steads and the life-style which they represent.

Notes to Chapter Eight

1. K. D. White, *Roman Farming*, p. 436ff and A. G. McKay, *Houses, Villas and Palaces in the Roman World*.
2. E. Gjerstad, *Early Rome*, III, p. 53ff and figs. 23-26, cf. fig. 6 above, p. 116.
3. Dion. Hal. I, 79, 11; Plutarch, Romulus, 20; Vitruvius, II, 1, 5.
4. A. Boethius, *The Tomb with the Thatched Roof at Cerveteri*, *Opuscula Romana*, Vol. VI, 1968, p. 15.
5. Boethius, op. cit., p. 19.
6. C. E. Ostenberg, *Luni sul Mignone e Problemi della Prehistoria d'Italia*, p. 40. For the dating, see p. 63.
7. C. E. Ostenberg, *Case etrusche di Acquarossa*, Rome, 1975.
8. A later version of this 'wattle and daub' was the *opus craticium* mentioned by Vitruvius, 11, 8, 20.
9. Ovid, *Met.* V, 447-8, cf. Virgil, *Aen.* VIII, 456.
10. cf. Pliny, *N.H.* XIV, 5 (46): 'quas suspendas duracinas Aminias maiores, vel ad fabrum ferrarium pro passis hae recte conduntur.' Also Petronius, *Satyricon*, 135.
11. Cato, CLXII, 3; Col. XII, 55, 3: 'in carnario suspendi, quo modicus fumus perveniat', et passim.
12. For a shepherd's hut built of reeds, without stonework, see the water colour by J. R. Cozens (1752-1797) of a hut near Gaeta, S.

Italy. (Victoria and Albert Museum, no. 84, 1894.)

13. *Memoirs of the American Academy in Rome,* Vol. IV, 1924, Plates IV and VIII.

14. Hellenistic examples are discussed by Jan Pečírka, *Homestead Farms in Classical and Hellenistic Hellas,* in *Problèmes de la Terre en Grèce ancienne,* ed. M. I. Finley, p. 123 and 128. P. W. Lehmann, *Roman Wall Paintings from Boscoreale,* Cambridge, Mass., 1953, on pp. 99-100 discusses in particular the tower house with the sloping roof which appears in some of the paintings. He compares it with a standard type of rural dwelling in Campania which has continued in use well into the present century. Lehmann draws a distinction between the tower-dwelling and towers which were used as storehouses or look-outs.

15. For other pictures of buildings see M. I. Rostovtzeff, *Die hellenistisch — römische Architekturlandschaft,* Röm. Mitt. XXVI (1911) pp. 1-185.

16. PBSR XVII, 1962, p. 179.

17. PBSR XVIII, 1963, p. 147.

18. For outbuildings belonging to the villa at Bignor, their size and arrangement, see S. Applebaum, *Some Observations on the Economy of the Roman Villa at Bignor, Sussex, Britannia,* Vol. VI, 1975. This is a large *villa rustica,* but details concerning the farmyard and buildings have relevance to our subject. Applebaum considers the possibility that storage space on the home farm may have been available for tenants' produce.

CHAPTER NINE

The Equipment of the Peasant Cultivator

Small rural dwellings of the kind which have been considered in the previous chapter must have been sparsely furnished, and their contents can be estimated from descriptions extant in the works of the Roman poets, as well as from Cato's lists of farm equipment. As the basic necessities of everyday living indoors can have differed little in the urban situation, discoveries at Pompeii, Herculaneum and Ostia, together with comments in Martial, Petronius and Juvenal will help us to complete the picture. Recent discoveries at Herculaneum, however, suggest that the amenities enjoyed by lower and middle class inhabitants of towns may sometimes have been superior to those which existed in small country dwellings.[1] The lists which Cato provides (ch. X and XI) are intended to describe the requirements both of household equipment and farm implements for an olive plantation of 240 *iugera* (ch. X) and for a vineyard of 100 *iugera* (ch. XI). Although these are larger holdings than those which we are discussing, the type of provision deemed necessary for farm workers would be based on that which was usual at the time for the various gradations of the rural population.

It is clear from Cato (Ch. XIII) that free workers were considered to require better sleeping accommodation than slaves. A study of the lists reveals that the *vilicus* and *vilica* and the free or permanently employed hands occupied between them the eight available beds, which were of two different types. Four of these were *lecti*, including one which was in a separate room, four were wooden frames with thongs stretched over them. The *lecti* were presumably beds with solid frames filled in with wooden slats, as found at Herculaneum. All had mattresses and coverlets. At the vineyard (ch. XI) if the same arrangement applies, the ten *operarii* (who may be day-labourers only, or slaves) had no beds provided, but the six other employees occupied between them four beds, with mattresses and coverlets. As we have noted with respect to rations, Cato's provision for employees may sometimes have been more generous than that available to self-employed farmers on the poverty line. Martial (XI, 32) catalogues the household equipment which even a poor man would possess, but which the unfortunate Nestor lacks: a toga, a hearth, a bug-ridden bed, a rush mat, a lock and key and a cup.[2] A similar account may be found in Martial, XI, 56. A different word is used here for the bed, *grabatus*,[3] suggesting a contrivance less comfortable than those mentioned by Cato, and the Stoic owner sleeps in his toga. In Martial XII, 31, Vacerra is moving house, with a bed, a table, a lantern and a wooden bowl. The bed might have a *stragulus* on it (XIV, 148) or a mattress stuffed with chopped reeds (XIV, 160). With the addition of a water jar and other earthenware containers and sometimes a storage chest, these constituted the essential furnishings of a poor home, whether in town or country.

If household furniture was scanty, the utensils and implements of the steading, 'σκεύη παντοῖα, οἶς γῆ τ'ἐξεργάζεται καὶ καρποὶ συγκομίζονται', (Dion, Hal. VII, 87, 5) were numerous and varied. A large proportion of them were wholly or partly of wood or other perishable materials. The amount of metal used for tools and vessels on the ancient Italian farm would vary with its availability in a particular area and with the affluence of the proprietor. The word *ferramenta* is used (often in a collective sense) to denote iron implements as distinct from those made of wood, and in this respect it forms a contrast to the use of *ferrum* and σίδηρος for weapons, for these are employed to distinguish iron from bronze. *Ferramenta* shows its precise meaning when used for example by Cato (II, 7): he advises selling 'ferramenta vetera'. Wooden tools would not be sold, as they were made on the farms and when worn out would be broken or useless. A passage of Columella (II, 10, 27) contains a hint of the superstition with which iron tools were originally regarded. He is discussing the cultivation of medick as a fodder plant. 'Post sationem ferro tangi locus non debet; atque, ut dixi, ligneis rastris sariendus et identidem runcandus est . . .' There is a good reason for avoiding the use of iron tools here, because damage to plants must be kept to a minimum when weeding, but the way in which the prohibition is expressed suggests something in the nature of a taboo.

From our point of view today metal is very conspicuous because of archaeological discoveries. The innumerable digging tools, sickles, knives and plough shares found on Roman sites throughout Italy and other parts of the Roman Empire testify to the widespread use of iron for these purposes. Even in the case of the metal knife, however, which seems a most desirable acquisition and for which other materials form very inadequate substitutes, there are distinct reminiscences in Latin literature of other expedients. Examples of this are the flint knife used for killing sacrificial victims, and the use of reeds for cutting up food: also for cutting down or ploughing up bracken (Pliny *N.H.* XVIII, 8 (45)). Throughout the Roman period many tools which could be made of iron were also produced in wood, for example the *pala lignea*[4] and the hay fork. Georges Duby (*The Early Growth of the European Economy*, p. 15) dealing with a much later period, considers that from the sixth to eighth century AD the amount of iron in agricultural equipment was extremely limited. At that time most of the peasants' own tools, as distinct from those supplied by the owners for work on large estates, were of wood, including their ploughs. He thinks that even the large monastic estates were backward in equipping farms because of respect for classical models. He continues: 'Because Roman civilisation was a predominantly Mediterranean one, because the Mediterranean is poor in metals, because arable soils there are thin, and because ploughing did not involve turning over the soil but merely breaking its upper crust and destroying the weeds, the Romans had scarcely concerned themselves with improving ploughing techniques . . .' Some of the conditions which Duby mentions affect other techniques besides ploughing, and his remarks probably have some relevance to the period we are discussing. Wood and wicker were utilised in great quantity at any rate for the minor equipment of a peasant holding in the Roman period. When we have studied the farm equipment of the smallholder we can well understand why Pliny opens Book XVI of his *Natural History* by questioning how a tribe can exist if it has no trees.

The iron tools, sickles, pruning-knives, spades, hoes, could be bought at the local market or from the smith who made them. The more affluent farmer might go some distance to obtain the best, as Cato suggests when he lists the places where various items of equipment should be bought (*De Agri Cultura* CXXXV). Iron tools, he advises, should be bought at Cales and Minturnae, carts and sledges at Suessa and in Lucania, yokes in Rome. Buckets and copper vessels should be obtained at Capua and Nola.[5] But he realises that an implement such as a plough will only be suitable for the local conditions: Roman ploughs will be good for heavy soil, Campanian for dark loam. All these tools, together with baskets, lamps, millstones and the whole equipment of a farm would be passed on from father to son, in some cases for many generations. This is one of the reasons why the basic patterns change so little through the centuries. Items would only be bought if the family was enlarged sufficiently to need them or the article was worn out or broken. Mention of the 'wear and tear' of equipment is common in contracts, as in Cato CXLIV, 1, of ladders, and CXLVI, 3, of all the apparatus necessary for harvesting and processing olives. The phrase 'quae vetustate fracta erunt' sounds as if it was part of the established formula of such transactions. The farmer did not mind using a broken tool, however, as is suggested by Columella's mention in Book X, 89, of using 'fracti dente ligonis' instead of a *marra*. This is in the context of the villa farming of the Empire.[6] In considering the details of a subsistence economy it is important to appreciate the amount of necessary equipment which is inherited from previous generations. Many of the vessels and implements would have little or no monetary value, being made or adapted rather than purchased. Nevertheless they were essential to the work of the farm, and could not all have been immediately acquired if not ready to hand.

The following is a list of the minimum equipment which would be possessed by an Italian smallholder in the Roman period. Items bracketed would not be found on every farm: their presence would depend upon the activities pursued there. Articles containing a considerable proportion of wood or other perishable substance, leaving little trace for the archaeologist, are starred.

*plough	*flat trays for	lamps and lanterns
hoe	carrying	knives
rake	*rope	pruning knife
*shovel	(oil press)	scythe
spade	wine vat	(loom)
*dibble	handmill	bucket
*baskets	*broom	candlestick
*ladders	*sieve	milk-boiler
(yoke and harness)	*winnowing fan	poker ladles
jars and basins	(troughs)	axe saw
(beehives)	*hurdles	pestles and mortar
		milking-pail

It will be observed that on a small-holding where draught animals were not kept and the olive was not grown, at least one third of the articles in regular use by the cultivator are unlikely to have survived to the present day.

One of the noteworthy features of any such list of equipment is the widespread and varied use of wicker in ancient Italy. This surely originated with the smallholder, particularly in remote places where he was dependent upon his own resources for labour and craftsmanship, or in the uplands or dry heathlands where large trees were rare but brushwood plentiful. It suggests a scarcity of heavy iron tools, and in the case of small items such as strainers and muzzles, of skilled metal workers in the immediate locality of the farm. The continuation of its use on large estates and by countrymen working for wealthy owners was a survival of ancient custom, as well as a measure of economy at at time when labour was still plentiful, and small metal goods were hand-made and relatively expensive. On the type of farm with which we are concerned here the materials for basket-making were probably wild and would vary according to the locality, reeds, rushes and osier being used in damp, low-lying places, hazel and pliant branches in wooded country, broom and various dry shrubs in the uplands. A countryman might go some distance to procure the right materials, but all these are plentiful in Italy. *Spartium* (Spanish broom) is still used for basket-making in Mediterranean countries. It was evidently flattened by hammering before being used for certain purposes, because Columella, XII, 19, 4, specifically enjoins his readers not to use baskets made of 'sparto malleato' for straining must at vintage time. According to Pliny (*N.H.* XVI, 14(35)) bark was also used by countryfolk for making baskets, at any rate for the large, flat hampers used for carrying corn at harvest time and grapes at the vintage, and for making panniers. He mentions beech, lime, fir and pitch-pine, but he has already (13 (34)) discussed the cork-oak, which in certain areas must have been used for a variety of purposes. It is exploited commercially today, especially in Sardinia.

Virgil in *Georgics* I, line 266, says that baskets are made out of 'rubea . . . virga', that is, from the stems of the *rubus*, bramble. It seems strange that baskets should be made of this material unless a thornless variety was available. In *Farm Equipment of the Roman World* by K. D. White, Appendix B, M. Bonnington writes (p. 235) that there is evidence that the Romans hacked off the thorns with thorn-cutters so that brambles could be used for plaiting. On this he cites Columella (IV, 31, 1). However Columella is not discussing basketry here, but *vincula* — plant-ties and twine. The only hint he gives, which might suggest removing thorns, is the mention of 'maiorem operam', but this seems likely to refer to the greater difficulty of working with such intractable material, whether or not thorns are removed.[7] The two questions which arise in relation to the use of *rubus* for basket-making are: was this in fact a prickly plant, and does *rubus* in Latin include some other plants besides the bramble? Columella (XI, 2, 19) bids the farmer remove 'branches and brambles' from the cornfields ('ramos et rubos') and use them to form a hedge. Was he led away by the alliteration, or did brambles grow in the cornfields in sufficient quantity to be useful for hedging? Pliny (XVII, 13 (68)) thinks they were used for this purpose, for he writes of making hedges 'rubis depactis'. It would seem that the bush to which Roman writers give the name 'rubus' was usually regarded by them as being prickly. Columella (X, 1, 21) has:

> 'nec cruribus aequa
> terga rubi . . .'

Tibullus II, 9, 10 writes of 'hamatis . . . rubis'. Other examples are to be found in the Virgilian *Priapea*, III, 7-8, and in Ovid, *The Walnut Tree*, line 13. The word *rubus*, however, is often found in association with *sentis, vepres* and *dumus*. All three are used by Columella in XI, 3, 3-7, and they all include the same thorny plant, *paliurus* (Christ's thorn), which does make a good hedge. *Sentis* is properly the dog-rose or briar, but it is often used with *rubus* for thorny plants in general (as in Caesar, *De Bello Gallico* II, 17, 4). *Dumus* covers the same set of meanings but does not seem to have an exact connotation of its own, as the others have. In Virgil, *Georgics* III, 315, we find:

> 'horrentisque rubos et amantis ardua dumos'.

This line probably shows the correct use of *dumus*, that is for bushes which grow high up in mountainous country. These would not normally include the bramble. It is possible that *rubus* could be used by some authors on occasion as the equivalent of *dumus* for the various bushes found on heathland. It might also include other straggling plants such as clematis or smilax. As basket-making material all these suggest a local expedient used when nothing better was available. According to the literary evidence reeds as well as osiers were used for hard baskets, and this is in accord with the impression given by pictorial representations both ancient and modern.[8]

The lighter baskets or frails, used to contain cheese, were made either of broom, rushes or palm leaves. Their original purpose in connection with cheese-making was similar to that of strainers, which were also often made of wicker. As soon as the milk had curdled it was placed in wicker containers so that the whey could be drained off (Col. VII, 8, 3).[9] Reed baskets could also be used for drying the harder cheeses, as in the *Copa* of the *Appendix Vergiliana*, line 17:

'sunt et caseoli, quos iuncea fiscina siccat . . .'

In Virgil, *Eclogue* X, the *fiscella* has been woven of *hibiscus*. Other products which were strained through rush baskets were brine (Col. XII, 6), honey (IX, 15, 12), where a *saccus* is the alternative the juice of myrtle berries (XII, 38, 7), and vinegar (XII, 17, 2). Olives were put into a rush bag before pressing (Col. XII, 38, 7). The frails (*fisci*) could be washed in hot water and used again (XII, 52, 22).[10] On the use of wicker for sieves and strainers it is interesting to note the following parallel from nineteenth-century England (P. A. Wright, *Old Farm Implements*, p. 67): 'A whole variety of hand riddles and sieves were made, some being meshed with wood-splits, others with iron or stout wire'. Mats were also made of rushes, and these could be used to catch the olives as they fell from the trees (Col. XII, 52, 9), as polythene sheets are used nowadays. An unexpected use for osier twigs, and surely a country notion, is to be found in Virgil, *Georgics* III, line 166, where he suggests making collars for calves out of this material.

The wooden hurdle also had many uses about the farm. Cheeses were laid out to dry on hurdles (Palladius VI, 9). For drying figs they can be arranged to form an arched roof, like that of a *tugurium*, says Columella (XII, 15). They can be used for making pens for animals (Horace, *Epodes* II, 45) or woven fences (Virgil, *Georgics* II, 37). In contrast to the poorer countryman's use of the materials available, Columella (IV, 30) recommends the owner of a villa to plant chestnut trees so that hurdles can be made from their wood. Temporary huts could be made of a light wooden construction, and Palladius (I, 13) suggests using reeds for screens separating different parts of farm buildings. Trellises and wind-breaks could be made with branches, reeds and straw (Col. XI, 3, 63). Hurdles, with brushwood interlaced, could serve the purpose of a harrow (Virgil, *Georgics* I, 95; Col. II, 17, 4). From the hurdle probably came the wooden stretcher for carrying manure and other heavy loads (Cato XI, 4). René Dumont (*Types of Rural Economy*, p. 245) writing of a farm near Arezzo in Tuscany, des-cribes the same item as he had seen it in use: 'On this particular holding the métayer has no wheelbarrow, and so the manure is taken from the sheds and sheepfolds on a kind of stretcher carried by two men'. There is a picture of this being done in Roman times on the mosaic from Vienne already mentioned.[11] This contrivance is also discussed under the name of 'hand barrow' by P. A. Wright (*Old Farm Implements*, p. 66, fig. 33). The example illustrated was probably made for carrying heavy sacks, because the slats are wide apart and small objects would fall between them.[12]

The storage and preservation of the food produced is a funda-mental requirement in a subsistence economy and, while baskets were used for gathering the crops, most of them were stored in earthenware containers. Farms of all kinds appear to have had one or more *dolia* in the yard for the immediate supply of water: other jars, often sunk in the ground, sometimes secured by a concrete surround, held wine, oil, the various by-products of the vineyard and the olive grove, and certain dry commodities.[13] There is no specific name for a storage jar in Latin — at the harvest most of the available containers would be filled. The agronomists seem to regard the making of pottery as a professional task, not performed by the farmer or his labourers. They mend the jars and waterproof them, but do not make them. Varro (*R.R.* I, 2, 23) writes: 'ut neque lapidicinae neque harenariae ad agri culturam pertinent, sic figilinae.' A *figilina* could be a pit from which clay for tiles or bricks was dug, but the word is also used in connection with pottery. The complete dissociation of these activities from agri-culture on which Varro is insisting — for he compares the posi-tion to that of a farmer who happens to have an inn on his land — is more suitable to the pottery industry than to brick-making, which Palladius (VI, 12) regards as farm work. The making of pottery and tiles, unlike the production of sun-baked bricks, requires a kiln and a large quantity of wood to burn. The supply of wood consumed by an ancient farm was very considerable even without these activities. The use of a potter's wheel involved a skill which would at an early date mark out the *figulus* from others. Nevertheless, just as the keeping of an inn might augment the income of a farmer whose land was situated on a main thoroughfare, so the making and selling of pottery would have been a profitable side-line for a smallholder. Kilns for tile-making and sometimes for pottery have been found in some of the *villae rusticae*, and this is in accord with our literary evidence from Columella. Farmers are to order 'vasa idonea' to be prepared for storage purposes (XII, 4, 4). They evidently have control over the making of these, for they are to have wide mouths and the body of the jar is to be of the same width throughout. (XII, 4, 5). Columella's uncle had special dishes made for preserving grapes (XII, 44, 5). 'Creta figularis' was expected to be readily available, for in XII, 46, 7, it is to be used to cover fruit as a method of preserving it. On the large farm, therefore, we may expect that often some pottery was made, though Cato, CXXXV, gives advice about buying *dolia, labra* and tiles in the towns. The *Geoponika* contains a section entitled περὶ κατασκευῆς πίθων   (VI, 3) in which the type of clay required for pottery is discussed, and we are reminded that the larger vessels, in particular the *dolia*, are not made on a wheel, but the potters 'build them up' (ἐποικοδομοῦσι) on the ground in a warm room, a process taking several days. For this reason such jars were expensive, their price in the *Edict* of Diocletian being 1000 *denarii* each, which amounts to more than five weeks' wages for a farm worker according to the same regulations. This makes the *dolium* one of the items of farm property which the smallholder would hope to inherit from his forbears, and the abundant evidence we have for the mending of it and for its durability supports this. Cato (XXXIX) gives detailed instructions for mending *dolia* and examples of jars mended in this way have been found at Ostia and elsewhere.[14]

Among the most valuable items handed down from one generation of *rustici* to another were the ploughs, oil and wine presses and vats, yokes and copperware. Millstones and querns might also be inherited, especially if made from good, hard stone. There has been some discussion as to whether the donkey-mill or the rotary hand-mill came first into use in Italy in the Roman period.[15] The opinion of V. Gordon Childe seems to be widely accepted now, namely that the rotary hand-mill pre-dated the donkey-mill, because, quite apart from its probable domestic use, the hand-mill (*mola manualis*) was an essential part of the equipment of soldiers in the Roman army and must also have been used on merchant-ships. For a drawing of this type of hand-mill, with a rough wooden handle inserted, see A. Maurizio, *Histoire de L'Alimentation végétale*, p. 399, fig. 31. Figure 32 shows a similar device from a Roman relief in the Vatican Museum. The relation between the various methods of grinding corn in Roman times is summarised by R. J. Forbes (in *History of Technology*, ed. Charles Singer, Vol. II, p. 107): 'For centuries after the beginning of public bake-houses in Rome (third or second century BC) bread-making remained a major task for the housewife. In these circumstances the saddle-quern and various forms of grain-rubber remained in common domestic use long after more effective forms such as the pushing-mill and the rotary quern had been introduced'. Forbes connects the development of the portable rotary hand-mill with the army (p. 109). He also refers to the fact that the Roman word *pistor,* a baker, originally meant 'one who pounds in a mortar', since the mortar preceded the mill. Some such equipment as has been mentioned must have formed part of the peasant proprietor's inheritance or figured among his purchases in the market.[16] We must remember, however, that even for the small farmer the use of a good donkey-mill might be available on a shared basis ('si communiter pisunt', Cato CXXXVI), or he might take his grain to a *pistor* for this purpose. The quality and durability of the millstones available in different localities would vary greatly. A. J. Macleane, commenting on Horace, *Satires* I, 5, 91, remarks in his edition of 1853: 'The bread of Canosa is described by modern travellers to be as bad as ever. It is accounted for by the softness of the mill-stones'.

Literary evidence for the hardware associated with small-scale farming is scarce, for reasons stated by Vitruvius, *De Architectura* X, 1, 6: 'non minus quae sunt innumerabili modo rationes machinationum, de quibus non necesse videtur disputare, quando sunt ad manum cotidianae, ut sunt molae, folles fabrorum, raedae, cisia, torni ceteraque quae communes ad usum consuetudinibus habent opportunitates'. So much of the apparatus of daily living was not discussed by Roman writers because it was commonplace. Moreover in an era of slave-labour, when a sharp division existed between the life of the educated classes and that of the poorer workers even if they were free, there was little incentive for the study of everyday utensils and crafts.

In areas where the olive was cultivated even a small farm might have its *trapetum* or some other contrivance for pressing the olives and extracting the oil. Alternatively such equipment might be shared or used on a contractual basis. It seems likely that the *solea*, the *canalis* and the *tudicula*, which are named by Columella (XII, 52, 6-7) as devices inferior to the *trapetum*, were among those originally used by the *rustici* in some areas and later superseded. On small farms where space in the steading was very restricted, the accommodation of the standard type of oil-press with a beam twenty-five feet long (Cato XVIII, 2) would present a problem.[17] Yet Pliny (*N.H.* XVIII, 74 (317)) advocates the use of a pair, even if they are very large. Those who lived in areas where the olive did not grow, or who could not lay out the capital required to produce a supply of oil, obtained it from the market or, in remote places, used another vegetable oil as a substitute.[18] It is interesting that Columella in his discussion of oil production explicitly allows (XII, 52, 7) for variations of local custom and requirements: 'pro conditione tamen et regionum consuetudine'. He recurs to this idea in XII, 52, 10, 'si consuetudo erit regionis'.

On the subject of the wine-press Cato says very little. White (*Roman Farming*, p. 392) mentions two possible reasons for the omission of details of viticulture and concentration on olive-growing, namely that the growing of the olive on a large scale was a new feature in Italian agriculture at the time when Cato was writing, or that Cato's own interests were concentrated on the district of Venafrum, which was particularly suitable for the cultivation of the olive. Another reason might be that as yet many farmers were treading the grapes and did not use a wine-press. Since according to Vitruvius the wine-press needed an even longer press-beam than the *trapetum* (forty feet — see White, op. cit. p. 425) it was unlikely to find a place on a very small steading.

> 'musto feriet pede rusticus uvas,
> dolia dum magni deficiantque lacus',

writes Tibullus (II, 5, 85-6).

Treading the grapes was a popular motif in the art and literature of the Empire, and the most detailed account of it is the well-known description from the *Geoponika* (VI, 11). To show that it was not just a preliminary process directed to the purpose of separating the fruit from the stems, we may take a provincial example, from the New Testament, *Revelation* XIV, 19-20:

'So the angel put his sickle to the earth and gathered in its grapes, and threw them into the great winepress of God's wrath. The winepress was trodden outside the city, and for two hundred miles around blood flowed from the press to the height of the horses' bridles' (NEB).

It is probable that the smallholder in Italy often used this method without the pressing which followed it on the large estates. R. Billiard (*L'Agriculture dans l'Antiquité*, p. 235-6) wrotes: 'Au fond, il est parfaitement raisonnable de supposer que, dans l'enfance de la viticulture, il tint lieu de pressurage lui-même'. It is not quite clear what is meant here by 'l'enfance de la viticulture'. Does it mean the time when the vine first came into cultivation or all the time before it was cultivated on a commercial basis (or what Dion (*Histoire de la Vigne*) calls 'une viticulture de prestige')? If it means the latter, it will include all the early history of Rome.

The various types of plough used by the Romans are already well documented, as also are the designs of their hand-tools. The latter were doubtless more generally used by the smallholder, though draught animals may have been shared or hired when required, as is suggested by a passage of Justinian.[19] In addition to the difficulty of providing fodder for a yoke of oxen, many of the small plots available, often in hill-country, could not be cultivated with the plough. The importance of the mattock (*ligo* and *marra*) for the cultivation of marginal land should be noted. White (*Agricultural Implements of the Roman World*, p. 38) writes of it: 'In hilly areas it took the place of, or rather was not displaced by the plough'. Such implements must have been designed for striking hard or stony ground, and are still employed for this purpose in southern Europe today. They had other uses in viticulture on large Roman estates, but like most of the tools used there, owed their origin to an earlier and simpler type of husbandry. From a study of the passage cited by White (*Agricultural Implements*, pp. 94, 130-2, 158) it seems that only the *falx vinitoria* in its fully-developed form and the reaping-machine and certain types of plough were evolved during the large-scale farming activities of the late Republic and early Empire.

One further piece of equipment must be considered here, namely the loom, which might be expected to form part of the apparatus in use on the small farm. With regard to Roman Italy, however, there is some doubt about this. In *The Roman Economy* by A. H. M. Jones (ed. P. A. Brunt) we find the following comment upon the subject: 'How far the poor wove their own clothes we do not know, but the majority seem to have bought their garments' (p. 352). The reference is to the situation during the Empire, and some of the evidence is drawn from the *Edict* of Diocletian. A similar view is expressed by W. O. Moeller (*The Wool Trade of Ancient Pompeii*, Leiden, 1976, p. 6ff and p. 78) who is discussing the position in the first century AD. The literary and epigraphical evidence in Latin for home-weaving is scanty when compared with the amount available in Greek. Moreover in the Greek setting the literary references are supported by vase-paintings showing looms in use.[20] There is mention in Latin inscriptions of *vestiarii* in towns and markets, and *Digest* XIV, 3, refers to the pedlars or travelling salesmen whom they employed. How far from the urban areas these *institores* and *circitores* travelled is uncertain. Spinning and weaving at home would attract less attention though the well-known epitaph (ROL IV, 18) on Claudia who 'domum servavit, lanam fecit' suggests that spinning at any rate was one of the duties of a wife in the second century BC. Ovid, *Met.* VI, 53-69, describes in detail the process of weaving on a vertical loom, as also does Seneca, *Epist. Mor.* XC, but Ovid is writing in the context of Greek legend, and Seneca's only reference to contemporary practice concerns the luxury trade. At this time the two-beam vertical loom was beginning to supersede the warp-weighted loom, and it is the newer type which appears in the frieze from the Forum of Nerva in Rome, and in the wall-painting in the *hypogeum* of the Aurelii. Archaeological evidence for the warp-weighted loom is provided by the numerous loom-weights which have appeared on sites throughout Italy. Where these have been found in dwellings, rather than in temple precincts or tombs, they suggest the existence of a loom. There are as yet few examples known to have originated in small rural dwellings of the Roman period, though the loom-weights found in the house of Monte Sannace (Gioia del Colle, Apulia) indicate that cloth was woven by several families there (B. M. Scarfì, *Not. degli Scavi*, XVI, 1962, pp. 160-2). There were 70 loom-weights in a room of one house, 48 in another part of the same house, in another 48 of which 38 formed a single group. Another house contained 67. In one of the courtyards there were 88.[21] The date of these dwellings lies between 350 and 250 BC.[22] It seems likely that at this period and earlier weaving took place at home, at least in the more remote areas of Italy, and was associated with the pastoral mode of existence common at that time. This would form a parallel with the situation in Greece.[23] It may well have continued longer in some districts, if not on every farm, perhaps as a cottage industry.

Notes to Chapter Nine

1. J. E. Packer, *Middle and Lower Class Housing in Pompeii and Herculaneum: A Preliminary Survey*, in *Neue Forschungen in Pompeii*, B. Andreae and H. Kyrieleis, Recklinghausen, 1975, pp. 141-2.
2. cf. Juvenal, *Sat.* I, 3, 203-4, where Codrus owned a bed, a cupboard, a pitcher and a chest.
3. Essentially a portable contrivance as when St. Jerome uses it in the

Vulgate (to translate its Greek equivalent) for the mattress which the invalid, now cured, is asked to take away with him (Mark, II, 9). See also Seneca, *Epist. Mor.* XVIII, 7.

4. White, *Agricultural Implements of the Roman World*, p. 31.

5. Strabo, V, 2, mentions that wooden buckets come from Nuceria.

6. Virgil, *Georgics* II, 414-5. White (op. cit. pp. 38-9) has another explanation of 'fracti dente ligonis'. He thinks that it refers to a special type of *ligo* with a notched blade, known as a *fractus ligo*.

7. H. L. Edlin in *Woodland Crafts of Britain*, 1973, p. 116, suggests that the spiny outer skin was peeled off completely, rather than that thorns were removed one by one. This would leave a thin, pliant stem, which was used in Britain as a tying or binding material.

8. A basket which is probably made of reeds rather than withes appears in a painting (Naples, Museo Nazionale, 9909). It is filled with a substance which might be flour or curd cheese. In *Latina Tellus: La Campagna Romana* (A. Cervesato) p. 422, there is a photograph of a woman from the Alban Hills with a reed basket.

9. cf. the probable origin of the English word 'junket'.

10. Cato, LXVII, 'Fiscinas spongia effingat'.

11. Rostovtzeff, *Social and Economic History of the Roman Empire*, Vol. I (2nd edition, 1957) facing p. 216.

12. cf. the wooden transport sled from Amelia, N. Italy, in *Farm Implements for Arid and Tropical Regions*, by H. J. Hopfen, p. 41.

13. Hilgers, *Lateinische Gefässnamen*, pp. 172-3. W. F. Jashemski, *The Excavation of a Shop-House Garden at Pompeii, American Journal of Archaeology*, LXXXI (1977) describes the recent discovery of a *hortus* with seven *dolia* partially embedded in the ground. Broken lids were found near them. There was also a cistern and an area perhaps used for outdoor meals.

14. For Ostia, G. Gatti, *Not. degli Scavi*, 1903, p. 201: 'Alcuni dolii presentano rotture e screpolature anche assai lunghe, in vario senso, che fino da antico furono riparate per mezzo delle solite ricuciture con asticelle di piombo a forma di croce latina'. In the Ager Veientanus, PBSR, XXIII, 1968, p. 130.

15. V. Gordon Childe, *Rotary Querns on the Continent and in the Mediterranean Basin, Antiquity* XVII (1943), p. 19.

16. In E. C. Curwen, *Querns, Antiquity* XI (1937) Plate III (facing page 136) there is a photograph of a rotary quern in use on the Isle of Foula (Shetland) in 1902; cf. p. 149, fig. 39, a modern Scottish quern from N. Uist, showing the method of adjustment for grinding fine or coarse meal. Domestic and military types of quern from the Roman period are also discussed but only with British examples.

17. Though Cato LXVIII does tell us to raise the press-beam to the roof and hang the ropes on it.

18. Pliny, *N.H.* XV, 7 (24-32) lists various other vegetable oils; it is noticeable that Gubbio in the Apennines is mentioned as using one of them. Strabo, *Geographia* IV, 6, 2, says that the Ligurians obtained olive oil from Genoa in exchange for their own produce. These were also people from a mountain region.

19. *Institutes*, XXIV, p. 234 (ed. Thomas, 1975). The idea of two farmers who each own one ox, sharing them, is being used to illustrate a legal point.

20. G. R. Davidson, *Hesperia*, Suppl. VII, 1943; A. di Vita, *Sui pesi da telaio: una nota, Archeologia classica*, Vol. VIII, 1956, p. 40.

21. Scarfî, p. 160, remarks: 'I telai antichi sembra avessero da 50 a 70 pesi e quindi almeno in tre casi avremmo la fornitura completa di un telaio'. A deposit of loom-weights was also found on the acropolis of Satrianum (R. R. Holloway, *Satrianum*, 1970).

22. Scarfî, p. 160.

23. G. R. Davidson, *Hesperia*, Suppl. VII, 1943, and P. Zancani Montuoro, *L'Edificio quadrato nello Heraion alla foce del Sele*, in *Atti della Società Magna Grecia*, VI-VII (1965-6).

CHAPTER TEN

Conclusion

While many questions concerning subsistence farming in the Roman period must necessarily remain open, it seems that certain conclusions can be drawn within the limits of present knowledge. First, the subject of ancient farming must be discussed with reference to Italy as a whole, and not merely to the *ager publicus* or the *coloniae*. We have seen that a considerable proportion of the small farms in Italy throughout the Roman period must have been in hill-country and on marginal land. Varieties of climate and terrain produced wide divergences in the methods of farming, the crops grown, and the life-style of agricultural communities. Moreover it would be undesirable to confine the study of ancient agriculture to the large farm, to the commercial production of oil and wine, and the *latifundia*. If we are to understand fully the political and social history of Rome we must be aware of the modes of life pursued in the countryside by thousands of her citizens and 'allies', and of the changes, however slight, which can be discerned in rural communities within the period of Rome's conquest and supremacy. Such changes, however, were often organisational and structural, leaving the basis of traditional procedures very little altered. Secondly, we cannot and should not make a sharp division between Roman farm life and those agricultural practices existing in Italy before or after the Roman period.

In relation to the villa farming of wealthy landowners the Romans built up a social structure and a technology which were to some extent peculiar to themselves, and these were confined mainly to the last two centuries BC and the first three centuries AD. But the methods and mode of life of the peasantry, the distribution of their settlements and the paths and tracks which led to them were developed before this period, and continued to be used long after it until they formed part of the rural life of the Middle Ages. At the same time it should be observed that in the Roman period the type of husbandry practised on the large farm and the smallholding had much in common. Ultimately the explanation of this lies in the fact that the Romans in Italy were not alien conquerors imposing exotic ideas upon a subjugated population: rather their strong military and political power was built upon an indigenous agricultural and pastoral tradition. The owner of the villa was drawing upon a fund of knowledge and practice built up by generations of small farmers. Some of this tradition was mediated to him through his family, his workers or his neighbours: some he may have learnt from the written sources which have come down to us. Although, however, peasant farming should be considered in relation to a generous time-scale, it is subject to strict geographical limitations. While the methods of Roman commercial enterprise, in farming as in other departments of life, affected profoundly those of other Mediterranean countries, and of Europe even as far north as Britain, the expedients of the poorer Italian cultivators were not so readily exported.

Peasant agriculture in Italy was essentially regional in character and this is one of the features which emerge most clearly from any study of it. In the far south of Italy there are the special problems of an arid zone, which must already have been apparent in ancient times, even if not so urgent as they are today. Coastal settlements throughout the length of the peninsula had a life of their own, often combining maritime pursuits with agriculture. The sparse population of the mountainous regions was at all times engaged upon 'attività agrosilvopastorali', to adopt the inimitable Italian phrase (*Quaderno del Parco nazionale d'Abruzzo*, 5, p. 7). It is true that local influences bore more heavily upon the smallholder than upon his wealthier contemporaries, who achieved greater mobility and wider contacts. But in the basic operations undertaken from day to day by the farm-worker, the methods, and most of the tools, were those of the 'small man'. With regard to land holdings, there has been much discussion of the two *iugera* allocations, but the most important point to note in the earlier period is the existence of these allocations at all. Nothing could emphasize more clearly the change from a nomadic and pastoral existence to the pursuit of settled agriculture than the tradition of apportioning land to every citizen. It also bears clear reference to the time at which random clearance of vegetation and random occupation of plots first came under control. The laws concerning *occupatio* and *possessio* suggest that the reclaiming of derelict land and the appropriation of new areas for cultivation long continued, but with the increase of population and of urbanism such free-lance activities were gradually eliminated from the fertile lowlands.

Large settlements in most parts of Italy in the Roman period seem to have been closely associated with a *territorium*: the Roman colonial system followed in this respect an established pattern. Thus the development of urban centres as the domicile of a populace chiefly engaged in agriculture, which originated in the demands of defence and in the scarcity of level, cultivable land, was continued under the Romans and became a lasting feature of social organisation in Italy. This type of urban life, however, was not universal in Italy even during the period of Roman domination: there were also townships specialising in particular trades, crafts and products, most of them with some farms, market-gardens or smallholdings within their boundaries or in the immediate neighbourhood. Outlying farms were linked, if at all, to the urban or market centres by mule-tracks rather than by roads such as those which Strabo calls ʽἁμαξήλατοι' and transport of goods to and from the small farm was mainly by mule or donkey. When Varro says of mules: 'Hisce

enim binis coniunctis omnia vehicula in viis ducuntur' (II, 8, 5)
he is thinking of the main roads and urban areas. But there is a
remarkable eulogy of the 'asellus' in Columella VII, 1: it does not
need much fodder provided for it, and will eat even thorns, twigs
and chaff. It is 'plagarum et penuriae tolerantissimus' (VII, 2) —
and mention of 'penuriae' immediately links it with the small-
holding. Palladius, 'De Mulis et Asinis' (IV, 14, 4), perhaps echoing
this passage, writes: 'minor vero asellus maxime agro necessarius
est, qui et laborem tolerat et neglegentiam propemodum non
recusat'. In Apuleius, *Metamorphoses* VIII, 15, when the members
of Tlepolemus' household were making their escape, we are
reminded of the variety of loads which a pack animal carried:
'Gerebamus infantulos et mulieres, gerebamus pullos, passeres,
aedos, catellos et quidquid infirmo gradu fugam morabatur, nostris
quoque pedibus ambulabat'.

Inhabitants of scattered farms depended on the *nundinae* for
such purchases as they made, and these by their very name suggest
that they were intended to supplement the living of a farming
community which was largely self-sufficient. Being held every
eight days they did not, as did the shops and markets of the
towns, provide daily sustenance. The *nundinae* seem to a great
extent to be associated with the less affluent section of the population. Wealthy landowners, if they followed the precepts of Cato,
Varro and Columella, would have used them as little as possible
and discouraged their workers from frequenting them. The for-
tunes of the *nundinae*, therefore, would be likely to rise and fall
with those of the small farmers. Some indication of attitudes
toward this institution may be obtained from the history of the
word *nundinae* and its derivatives. While *nundinae* continued to
denote the 'market day', *nundinari* is frequently used in literature,
from the time of Cicero to that of the early Christian writers, in
a pejorative sense, implying either petty bargaining or a betrayal
of honour or ideals. *Nundinatio* was used in the same way, especially in the work of late authors such as Cassiodorus.

The market or fair could offer a temporary site for the exchange
of goods, permitting the nearest equivalent to a system of barter.
It also allowed the itinerant trader to produce his wares for sale in

a number of different centres. This was important when there was not a large demand for consumer durables within any one community. The markets also afforded opportunity for bargaining. It is often supposed that because official attempts at price regulation were made, as for example in Diocletian's *Edict*, all prices even in markets were fixed. In appointing maximum prices, Diocletian, as others had done before him, left room for bargaining where it was appropriate and customary. In relation to goods sold in this way the official price would be the starting-point. The trouble which Lactantius (*De Mortibus Persecutorum*, VII, 6-7) describes as having occurred 'ob exigua et vilia' would arise because the price-range within which buyer and seller could operate in bargaining was thus strictly controlled. Vendors therefore withheld their goods, using a sanction which has often been applied since in similar circumstances. Less well known than Diocletian's price code is the Greek inscription from Cyzicus (38 AD) where the δῆμος decrees that no seller 'πλειονος ἐπιβάλληται πιπράσκειν τῆς ἐνεστώσης τειμῆς', (*Sylloge Inscriptionum Graecarum*, 3rd edition, 799). One would expect 'πιπράσκῃ' but the addition of 'ἐπιβάλληται' in the sense of 'endeavour' surely suggests an 'asking price'? Examples of bargaining in Latin literature often refer to transactions in slave markets rather than the selling of commodities: these lead to more pertinent dialogue, as for instance in Plautus, *Persa* 549-672. Much of the interest of the story of the Sibyl bringing the prophetic books to Tarquin lies in its reversal of the normal bargaining situation. A fragment of Lucilius (*Saturae*, V, 164-6 Baehrens) is connected with the selling of produce:

'sicuti, cum primus ficos propola recentis
protulit et pretio ingenti dat primitus paucas,
at siccas ficos . . .'

The markets formed for the *rustici* their main contact with the outside world, and in so far as cultural changes, based on the urban centres did affect them, it was through the markets and the itinerant traders that they did so. Against this background the Roman achievement in unifying Italy is seen in all its magnitude. It is, however, easy to exaggerate the influence actually excercised by Rome over the lives of Italians in the less accessible parts of the peninsula, especially under the Republic.

We have noted the land hunger in Rome itself during the early Republic, when problems of distribution and settlement often concerned the quality and position of the holdings quite as much as their size. Peasant cultivators with their small plots of land formed at various periods an important element in the population of ancient Italy, yet during the Republic there are problems of identification concerning this group of people. Our sources for this period do not clearly distinguish between smallholders whose land, whether owner-occupied or rented, would seldom afford them adequate subsistence, and the more prosperous, and probably more articulate, group of working farmers who usually made a satisfactory living from their land. Such a distinction is probably reflected in accounts of the early census classes and of the criteria upon which the property qualifications for military service were based. Among the six classes supposed to exist originally (Dion. Hal. VI, 59, 2-8; Livy, I, 42-3; even Cicero *Republic* II, 22, 39, mentions five classes) at least two levels of income from subsistence farming must be represented. Dionysius himself distinguished betwen *proletarii* and a class above them 'πέμπτη δ'ἐκαλεῖτο συμμορία τῶν ὀλίγου πάνυ τετιμημένων ἀργυρίου' (VI, 59, 5). While the details regarding these classes cannot be pressed and their dating is uncertain, they indicate that a wide variety of levels of wealth and poverty was to be expected among Roman citizens during the Republican era, and the implications of this in practical terms have not always been appreciated. Assuming the existence of a class of small farmers making a modest but comfortable living, it is they who would have been more seriously affected by war conditions, veteran settlement and economic changes in general, as well as more likely to make their protests heard. For the post-Augustan situation Salvioli made a classification of rural society in Italy on the basis of legal phraseology (*Il Capitalismo antico*, Bari, 1929, p. 158). Under his fifth and last heading come 'coloni, rustici, rusticana plebs extra muros posita'. On any reckoning there remain in the lowest category the occupiers of *casae* and *tuguria* on marginal land; tenants of smallholdings; tillers of garden plots, searching for seasonal employment, often competing unsuccessfully with slave labour for work on the large estates. It is substantially this group, however, the least well provided, whose continuance as a section of the rural population can be most clearly discerned during the later years of the Roman Empire and the subsequent history of European agriculture.

Bibliography

ALFOLDI, András *Early Rome and the Latins*. Michigan, 1963.

ALVISI, Giovanna *La Viabilità romana della Daunia*. Bari, 1970.

ANDRÉ, Jacques *L'Alimentation et la cuisine à Rome*. Paris, 1961.

ASHBY, Thomas *The Roman Campagna in Classical Times*. Ed. J. B. Ward Perkins, London, 1970.

BADIAN, Ernst *Tiberius Gracchus and the beginning of the Roman Revolution*, in *Aufstieg und Niedergang der Römischen Welt*, I, 668-731, Berlin, 1972.

BARBIERI, Giuseppe *Osservazioni geografico-statistiche sulla transumanza in Italia. Rivista geografica italiana*, Vol. LXII, 1955.

BARKER, Graeme *The Economy of Medieval Tuscania: the Archaeological Evidence*. PBSR, Vol. XXVIII, 1973.

BERCHEM, Denis van *Les Distributions de Blé et d'Argent à la Plèbe romaine sous l'Empire*. Geneva, 1939.

BERNARDI, Aurelio *Nomen Latinum*. Pavia, 1973.

BILLIARD, Raymond *L'Agriculture dans l'Antiquité*. Paris, 1928.

BOETHIUS, Axel *Remarks on the Development of Domestic Architecture in Rome. American Journal of Archaeology*, XXXVIII (1934).

The Golden House of Nero. Michigan, 1960.

The Tomb with the Thatched Roof at Cerveteri. Opuscula Romana, VI, Lund, 1968.

BOETHIUS, A. and WARD PERKINS, J. B. *Etruscan and Roman Architecture*. Harmondsworth, 1970.

BONASERA, F., DESPLANQUES, H., FONDI, M. POETA, A. *La Casa rurale nell 'Umbria*. Ricerche sulle Dimore rurali in Italia, Vol. XIV.

BORDA, Maurizio *La Pittura romana*. Milan, 1958.

BOSERUP, Ester *The Conditions of Agricultural Growth: The Economics of Agrarian Change under Population Pressure*. London, 1965.

BRADFORD, J. S. P. *'Buried Landscapes' in Southern Italy*. *Antiquity*, XXIII, 1949.
The Apulia Expedition: An Interim Report. *Antiquity*, XXIV, 1950.

BRAUDEL, Fernand *The Mediterranean and the Mediterranean World in the Age of Philip II*. Vol. I. trans. S. Reynolds, London, 1972.
Capitalism and Material Life, 1400-1800. trans. M. Kochan. London, 1973.

BREHAUT, E. *Cato the Censor on Farming*. New York, 1933.

BROTHWELL, D. and P. *Food in Antiquity*. London, 1969.

BROWN, F. E. *Cosa I*. *Memoirs of the American Academy in Rome*, XX, 1951.

BRUNT, P. A. *The Army and the Land in the Roman Revolution*. JRS, Vol. LII, 1962.
Italian Manpower. Oxford, 1971.
Social conflicts in the Roman Republic. London, 1971.
Two Great Roman Landowners. *Latomus*, Vol. XXXIV, 1975.

BUCK, A. D. *A Grammar of Oscan and Umbrian*. New York, 1974.

BUCK, R. J. *The Via Herculia*. PBSR, Vol. XXXIX, 1971.

BURDESE, Alberto *Studi sull 'Ager Publicus*. Torino, 1957.

CARRIER, E. H. *Water and Grass*. London, 1932.

CASELLA, Domenico *La Frutta nelle pitture Pompeiane*, in *Pompeiana*. Naples, 1950.

CASTAGNOLI, Ferdinando *Le 'formae' delle colonie romane e le miniature dei codici dei gromatici*. Atti della reale Accademia d'Italia, Series VII, Vol. IV.

Orthogonal Town Planning in Antiquity. Massachusetts and London, 1971.

CERVESATO, Arnaldo *Latina Tellus: La Campagna romana.* Rome, 1910.

CHEVALLIER, Raymond *Roman Roads.* London, 1976.

CHISHOLM, Michael *Rural Settlement and Land Use.* London, 1962.

CIANFARANI, Valerio. *Trecentomila Anni di Vita in Abruzzo.* Chieti, 1962.

Culture adriatiche d'Italia. Rome, 1970.

Antiche Civiltà d'Abruzzo. Rome, 1969.

Clark, C. and Haswell, M. *The Economics of Subsistence Agriculture.* 3rd ed. London, 1967.

CLARK, J. G. D. *Prehistoric Europe: The Economic Basis.* London, 1952.

CLERICI, Luigi *Economia e Finanza dei Romani.* Bologna, 1943.

COLCHESTER Archaeological Group *Salt: The Study of an Ancient Industry.* ed. K. W. de Brisay and K. A. Evans. Colchester, 1975.

COLES, John *Archaeology by Experiment.* London, 1973.

COLONNA, Giovanni *Popoli e Civiltà dell'Italia antica,* Vol. 2. Rome, 1974.

CRAWFORD, M. H. *Roman Republican Coinage.* Vol. I, Cambridge, 1975.

CROISILLE, J.-M. *Les Natures mortes campaniennes.* Brussels, 1965.

CROVA, Bice *Edelizia e tecnica rurale di Roma antica.* Milan, 1942.

CURWEN, E. C. *Querns. Antiquity,* XI, 1937.

CURWEN, E. C. and HATT, G. *Plough and Pasture.* New York, 1953.

DE CUPIS, C. *Le Vicende dell 'Agricoltura e della Pastorizia nell' Agro romano.* Rome, 1911.

DEVOTO, Giacomo *Gli antichi Italici.* Florence, 1950.

DILKE, O. A. W. *Maps and Treatises of the Roman Land Surveyors. Geographical Journal,* Vol. CXXVII, part 4, 1961.

The Roman Land Surveyors. Newton Abbot, 1971.

Varro and the Origins of Centuriation. Atti del Congresso internazionale di Studi Varroniani. Rieti, 1976.

DIMBLEBY, G. W. *Plants and Archaeology.* London, 1967.

DION, Roger *Histoire de la Vigne et du Vin en France.* Paris, 1959.

DUBY, Georges *Rural Economy and Country Life in the Medieval West.* trans. C. Postan. London, 1968.

The Early Growth of the European Economy. trans. H. B. Clarke. London, 1974.

DUMONT, René *Types of Rural Economy.* London, 1957.

DUNCAN, Guy *Sutrium.* PBSR, Vol. XIII, 1958.

DUNCAN-JONES, R. *The Economy of the Roman Empire.* Cambridge, 1974.

EARL, D. C. *Tiberius Gracchus: A Study in Politics.* Coll. Latomus, LXVI, Brussels, 1963.

EARLE, Peter *Essays in European Economic History,* 1500-1800. Oxford, 1974.

EDLIN, H. L. *Woodland Crafts of Britain.* Newton Abbot, 1973.

FEA, D. C. *Storia delle Saline d'Ostia.* Rome, 1831.

FINLEY, M. I. *The Ancient Economy.* London, 1973.

FRANKLIN, S. H. *The European Peasantry.* London, 1969.

FREDERIKSEN, M. W. *Republican Capua.* PBSR, XIV, 1959.

Caesar, Cicero and the Problem of Debt. JRS, LVI, 1966.

FREDERIKSEN, M. W. and WARD PERKINS, J. B. *The Ancient Road Systems of the Central and Northern Ager Faliscus.* PBSR, XII, 1957.

GABBA, Emilio *Le Origini dell'Esercito professionale in Roma: i Proletarii e la Riforma di Mario. Athenaeum,* XXVII, 1949.

Motivazioni economiche nell'Opposizione alla Legge di Tib. Sempronio Gracco, in *Polis and Imperium* ed. J. A. S. Evans, Toronto, 1974.

Mercati e Fiere nell'Italia romana. Studi classici e orientali, XXIV, 1975.

GENIERE, J. de la *Aspetti e Problemi dell'Archeologia del Mondo indigeno,* in *Le Genti non Greche della Magna Grecia.* Naples, 1972.

GIEROW, P. G. *The Iron Age Culture of Latium,* Vol. I and II. Lund, 1964 and 1966.

GJERSTAD, Einar *Early Rome.* Vol. III, Lund, 1960.

GORDON CHILDE, Vere *Rotary Querns on the Continent. Antiquity,* XVII, 1943.

GRIMAL, Pierre *A la Recherche de L'Italie antique.* Paris, 1961.

HARRIS, W. V. *Rome in Etruria and Umbria.* Oxford, 1971.

HEITLAND, W. E. *Agricola.* Cambridge, 1921.

HEURGON, Jacques *The Daily Life of the Etruscans.* trans. J. Kirkup. London, 1964.

HILGERS, Werner *Lateinische Gefässnamen.* Düsseldorf, 1969.

HINRICHS, F. T. *Die Geschichte der gromatischen Institutionen.* Wiesbaden, 1974.

HOPFEN, H. J. *Farm Implements for Arid and Tropical Regions.* United Nations F.A.O., Rome, 1960.

HUGGETT, F. E. *The Land Question and European Society.* London, 1975.

ISAAC, Erich *The Geography of Domestication.* New Jersey, 1970.

JASNY, Naum *The Wheats of Classical Antiquity.* Baltimore, 1944.

The Daily Bread of the Greeks and Romans. Osiris, IX, 1950.

JONES, A. H. M. *The Roman Economy.* ed. P. A. Brunt. Oxford, 1974.

JONES, G. D. B. *Capena and the Ager Capenas.* PBSR, XVII, 1962, and XVIII, 1963.

Civil War and Society in Southern Etruria, in *War and Society,* ed. M. R. D. Foot, London, 1973.

LATOUCHE, Robert *The Birth of Western Economy.* trans. E. M. Wilkinson. London, 1961.

LE GALL, J. *Le Tibre dans l'Antiquité.* Paris, 1953.

LEVICK, Barbara *Roman Colonies in Southern Asia Minor.* Oxford, 1967.

McKay, A. G. *Houses, Villas and Palaces in the Roman World.* London, 1975.

MACMULLEN, Ramsay *Enemies of the Roman Order.* Harvard, 1976.

Market-Days in the Roman Empire. Phoenix, XXIV, 1970.

MAGALDI, Emilio *Lucania Romana.* Part I. Rome, 1947.

MAGI, Filippo *Il Calendario dipinto sotto S. Maria Maggiore.* Vatican City, 1972.

MAIURI, Amedeo *Ercolano. I Nuovi Scavi.* (1927-58). Rome, 1958.

MAU, August *Pompeii: its Life and Art.* trans. F. W. Kelsey, New York, 1899.

MAURIZIO, Adam *Histoire de l'Alimentation végétale depuis la Préhistoire jusqu'à nos jours.* trans. F. Guidon. Paris, 1932.

MAURON, Marie *La Transhumance du Pays d'Arles aux grandes Alpes.* Paris, 1951.

MEIGGS, Russell *Roman Ostia.* 2nd edition, Oxford, 1973.

MERTENS, J. *Alba Fucens I.* Brussels and Rome, 1969.

MINTO, A. *Due Pozzi granari in Località a Cinigiano* (Grosseto). *Not. degli Scavi,* Vol. XII, 1936.

MORITZ, L. A. *Grain Mills and Flour in Classical Antiquity.* Oxford, 1958.

MUHLY, J. D. *Copper and Tin.* Transactions of the Connecticut Academy of Arts and Sciences, Vol. XLIII, 1973.

MUSTO, Dora *La Regia Dogana della Mena delle Pecore di Puglia.* Rome, 1964.

NENQUIN, Jacques *Salt: A Study in Economic Prehistory.* Bruges, 1961.

NEUBERGER, Albert *The Technical Arts and Sciences of the Ancients.* trans. H. L. Brose. London, 1930.

NICE, Bruno *Per uno studio geografico dei mercati periodici della Toscana. Rivista geografica italiana,* Vol. 62, 1955. Florence.

OSTENBERG, C. E. *An Etruscan Archaic House-Type not described by Vitruvius.* Opuscula Romana, Vol. VII, Acta Instituti Romani Regni Sueciae, Ser. I, XXX.

Luni sul Mignone e Problemi della Preistoria d'Italia. Lund, 1967.

Case etrusche di Acquarossa. Rome, 1975.

OVERBECK, J. A. *Pompeji,* Vol. II, Leipzig, 1866.

PACKER, J. E. *The Insulae of Imperial Ostia.* Rome, 1971.

PERCIVAL, John *The Roman Villa.* London, 1976.

PETERS, W. J. T. *Landscape in Romano-Campanian Mural Painting.* Assen. 1963.

PLANTA, R. von *Grammatik der Oskisch-Umbrischen Dialekte.* Vol. II, Strassburg, 1897.

PLOMMER, Hugh *Vitruvius and Later Roman Building Manuals.* Cambridge, 1973.

POSTAN, M. M. *The Medieval Economy and Society.* London, 1972.

POTTER, T. W. *A Faliscan Town in South Etruria.* London, PRETE, M. and FONDI, M. *La Casa rurale nel Lazio settentrionale.* Florence, 1957.

PUGLISI, S. M. *La Civiltà appenninica.* Florence, 1959.

RIZZO, G. E. *Monumenti della Pittura antica scoperti in Italia.* Rome, 1936.

ROSTOVTZEFF, M. I. *Die hellenistisch — römische Architektur-landschaft. Rom. Mitth.* XXVI, 1911.
Social and Economic History of the Roman Empire. 2nd edition, Oxford, 1957.

SALMON, E. T. *Samnium and the Samnites.* Cambridge, 1967.
Roman Colonization under the Republic. London, 1969.

SAUER, C. O. *Agricultural Origins and Dispersals.* American Geographical Society, Cambridge (Mass.) 1952.

SERENI, Emilio *Communità rurali nell 'Italia antica.* Rome, 1955.
Storia del Paesaggio agrario Italiano. Bari, 1961.

SHERWIN-WHITE, A. N. *The Roman Citizenship.* Oxford, 1939.

SIRAGO, V. A. *L'Italia agraria sotto Traiano.* Louvain, 1958.

SKYDSGAARD, J. E. *Varro the Scholar.* Analecta Romana Instituti Danici, Suppl. IV. Copenhagen, 1968.

SWINBURNE, Henry *Travels in the Two Sicilies in the years 1777-80.* Vols. I and II. London, 1783-5.

THOMSEN, Rudi *The Italic Regions.* Copenhagen, 1947.
Early Roman Coinage. Vol. III, Copenhagen, 1961.

TIBILETTI, G. F. *Ricerche di Storia agraria romana. Athenaeum,* XXVIII (1950).

TILLY, Bertha *Varro the Farmer.* London, 1973.

TOYNBEE, A. J. *Hannibal's Legacy.* Vols. I and II. Oxford, 1965.

TOZZI, P. *Storia padana antica.* Milan, 1972.

TRUMP, D. H. *Central and Southern Italy before Rome.* London, 1966.

VIRONE, L. E. *Borgo a Mozzano. Technical Assistance in a Rural Community in Italy.* World Land Use Survey, Occasional Papers No. 4, Bude, 1963.

WARD PERKINS, J. B. *Etruscan and Roman Roads in Southern Etruria.* JRS, Vol. XLVII, 1957.

Landscape and History in Central Italy. Oxford, 1964.

Cities of Ancient Greece and Italy. London, 1974.

WESTRUP, C. W. *Introduction to Early Roman Law.* Vols. I-IV. Copenhagen and London, 1934-1950.

WHITE, K. D. *Agricultural Implements of the Roman World.* Cambridge, 1967.

Roman Farming. London, 1970.

Farm Equipment of the Roman World. Cambridge, 1975.

Country Life in Classical Times. London, 1977.

WIRTH, Fritz *Römische Wandmalerei.* Darmstadt, 1968.

WISEMAN, T. P. *Roman Republican Road Building.* PBSR, Vol. XXXVIII, 1970.

WONTERGHEM, F. van *Le Culte d'Hercule chez les Paeligni: Documents anciens et nouveaux. L'Antiquité classique*, XLII, 1973, fasc. I.

WRIGHT, P. A. *Old Farm Implements.* London, 1961.

ZANCAN, Leandro *Ager Publicus.* Padua, 1935.

ZEHNACKER, Hubert *Moneta: Recherches sur l'Organisation et l'Art des Émissions monetaires de la Republique romaine.* Rome, 1973.

Index of Latin Words

General Index